CHEROKEE THOUGHTS,
HONEST AND UNCENSORED

Cherokee Thoughts, Honest and Uncensored

ROBERT J. CONLEY

UNIVERSITY OF OKLAHOMA PRESS: NORMAN

Also by Robert J. Conley

The Witch of Goingsnake and Other Stories (Norman, 1988)
Ned Christie's War (New York, 1990)
Mountain Windsong: A Novel of the Trail of Tears (Norman, 1992)
Nickajack (New York, 1992)
War Woman: A Novel of the Real People (New York, 1997)
Brass (New York, 1999)
Cherokee Dragon: A Novel of the Real People (New York, 2000)
Medicine War (New York, 2001)
Sequoyah (New York, 2002)
(with David G. Fitzgerald) *Cherokee* (Portland, 2002)
Cherokee Medicine Man (Norman, 2003)
The Cherokee Nation : A History (Albuquerque, 2005)
A Cherokee Encyclopedia (Albuquerque, 2007)

Library of Congress Cataloging-in-Publication Data

Conley, Robert J.
  Cherokee thoughts, honest and uncensored / Robert J. Conley
      p.   cm.
  Includes index.
  ISBN 978-0-8061-3943-2 (pbk. : alk. paper)
  1. Cherokee Indians—History. 2. Cherokee Indians—Social conditions. 3. Cherokee Indians—Attitudes. I. Title.
  E99.C5C7164 2008
  970.004'97—dc22

                                                        2008005819

The paper in this book meets the guidelines for permanence and durability of the Committee on Production Guidelines for Book Longevity of the Council on Library Resources. ∞

1 2 3 4 5 6 7 8 9 10

Contents

Acknowledgments — vii

Introduction — 3

Indian Casinos — 6

Ricochet — 15

Stand Watie and the Treaty of 1866 — 18

Cherokee Wannabes — 33

Oklahoma — 40

All Indians Are Alike, or "Chiefing" — 45

Cherokee Outlaws — 49

Grafters, Sooners, and Other Crooks — 66

Why the DAR Did Not Like Me — 70

Cherokee Women and the Clan System — 75

Henry Starr — 81

Cherokee Literature — 87

Cherokee Celebrities — 96

Indian Humor — 102

The Five Civilized Tribes — 110

Cherokee Names — 114

Will Rogers: Cherokee Writer and So Much More — 121

Linking Back — 129

Contents

The Freedmen Controversy   133

John Oskison and Me   145

Cherokee Cards   151

Keetoowah   154

The Dragging Canoe–Nancy Ward Controversy   158

California Cherokees   161

Tribally Specific Historical Fiction   164

Cherokees and Sports   174

Parris: My Cherokee Family   185

Old-Time Cherokee Warriors: Charlie Wickliffe,
    the Army Corps of Engineers, and the Port of Catoosa   190

Notes   193

Index   197

Acknowledgments

"Ricochet"
was published in *True West* (July 1991).

"Oklahoma"
was published in *Aboriginal Voices: A Native North American News Magazine* (May–June 1999).

"Cherokee Outlaws"
is a slightly revised version of Robert J. Conley, "Cherokees on the Scout," which originally appeared in the *Roundup* 32, no. 10 (November–December 1984): 11–20. In its present form, it was delivered to a Cherokee Nation History Symposium in Tahlequah, Oklahoma, in 1993.

"Linking Back"
Most of this essay was originally published as the beginning of the text of *Cherokee*, published by Graphic Arts Center Publishing in 2002, with photography by David Fitzgerald, and is reprinted here, with minor revisions, by their kind permission. The final paragraph is a newly written conclusion and did not appear in the book.

CHEROKEE THOUGHTS,
HONEST AND UNCENSORED

Introduction

This collection of essays deals with various Cherokee subjects, some historical and some contemporary. There are considerations of the lives of famous people, of historical events, of contemporary practices. Some essays deal with subjects that are unfamiliar to most readers today. Some are on subjects about which most readers have already formed opinions. Indian casinos come quickly to mind here. Everyone has an opinion, whether educated or uneducated. All, however, are subjects that can be researched fairly easily.

I have been a writer on Cherokee subjects for nearly forty years, writing mostly historical fiction. Because of that, I have done a great deal of research into Cherokee matters. More recently, I have been writing nonfiction, including a history of the Cherokee Nation commissioned by the Cherokee Nation. I am Cherokee, and I have also spent countless hours talking to various Cherokee people on these and other subjects. We don't always agree with one another.

I am an individual, and I therefore have my individual take on these subjects, my personal opinion, if you will. Please keep in mind that I do not pretend to speak for the Cherokees. No one can do that. I speak for one Cherokee—me. Cherokees, like any group of people, have their own individual ideas and thoughts and beliefs and prejudices. We do not all think alike. It is my opinion, I hope, that will be the main interest in this volume. For example, some people do know about Stand Watie, the Cherokee Confederate general and last Confederate general to surrender, but what do they think about General Watie? In my essay on General Watie, I will tell you how I feel about him, and I'll tell you why I feel that way. The same with the phenomenon of "chiefing" that is practiced in Cherokee, North Carolina. I'll tell you what it is, in case you don't already know, and what I think about it. The issue of the Cherokee Freedmen is much in the news these days and is quite controversial. If you read this book, I'll tell you where I stand. And for you fans of the University of Oklahoma Sooners, I have some food for thought.

The essays' topics come from the Cherokee Nation, the Eastern Band of Cherokee Indians, the United Keetoowah Band of Cherokee Indians (that is, the three federally recognized Cherokee tribes), the state-recognized tribes, the totally unrecognized groups, and individuals, both those enrolled or registered and those "uncarded," as they say. Most of my topics, however, do come from Oklahoma. That is my home. That is where I am enrolled (with the United Keetoowah Band), and that is where most of my experience arises.

I won't claim to cover every topic of interest to Cherokees or to people interested in things Cherokee, but I believe I cover a great many of them. These are the topics that come most readily to my mind, that are closest to my heart, or have been most in the news. I hope that my readers will find them of some interest. I know that I will aggravate some and will downright anger others. Essays are by nature personal, if not private, and personal writing, if anything, should be even more honest than other kinds of writing. So I have been honest, leaving room for a bit of sarcasm, of course. That is not to say I have been truthful or I am right. Where facts are concerned, I have been as factual as I know how to be, as truthful as possible. But overall, I have been honest. I have given my opinion on these matters. People with honest opinions can disagree with one another. If I have to leave the state following publication of this book, so be it. But I don't think that will happen.

Cherokees today come in all shapes and fashions. There is what I like to think of as the core of Cherokee culture, the full-blood, mostly traditional, mostly bilingual Cherokees, and even these come in three main categories. There are the Cherokees who participate in stomp dances; there are those who attend the Cherokee churches, mostly Baptist; and there are those who see no conflict and attend both. If you think of the Cherokee core as the place where a pebble hits the water, then think of all the ripples that spread out from there. The Cherokee ripples spread out until we have on the outermost ring people who are for all practical purposes white people, but who have a very small fraction of Cherokee blood, no knowledge of Cherokee history or culture, and no real contact with other Cherokee people. And Cherokees are used to controversy; in fact, they enjoy it. Cherokees like to argue. That may be one reason there are so damn many Cherokee lawyers.

Indian Casinos

In the last several years, any time I have been asked to speak to any group on any subject involving Indians—on anything from one of my own books to Cherokee history to Will Rogers to anything at all about Indians—when it comes to the question-and-answer period, someone always asks me about casinos. It seems like that is the only topic on anyone's mind anymore when they think about Indians. I don't know why it matters to anyone what I think about casinos, but it seems to matter to a good many people, so let's get it out of the way. What do I think about Indian casinos?

Not too many years ago, most Oklahomans would have thought you were crazy if you said that one day we would have casinos in Oklahoma. Today casinos seem to be on every corner. They are very controversial, but I love Indian casinos. I lose money in them sometimes, but sometimes I win. Oh, not large amounts, but enough to keep me interested. My friend Donnie Birchfield, a Choctaw, usually wins. Sometimes he wins big. Donnie cannot drive past an Indian casino without stopping, especially one he has not visited before. He claims that he's doing a study of them. I guess he really is, but I think the computer that runs his car is programmed to turn into the parking lot of any Indian casino. It sure takes a long time to drive across the state of Oklahoma with Donnie. As a matter of fact, a few years ago I made an automobile trip with Donnie. He was driving, and as we drove through Oklahoma on I40 going west out of Oklahoma City, Donnie stopped at every Indian casino we came across. It took us two days to get out of the state.

Indians have always been gamblers. Being Cherokee, of course, I know more about the Cherokees. The Cherokees were passionate gamblers in the early days, and they remain passionate gamblers.

Cherokees gambled on the outcome of various games, but one of the most popular in the early days was the game known widely as *chunkey*, but that's a Creek name. The Cherokees call it *gatayusti*. It was played with a throwing stick (a spear) and a stone disk. The player would get a running start, roll the stone disk, and then fling the stick after it. Ideally, when the stone stopped rolling, the stick would land and touch the stone. There were points given for how close the stick got to the stone. Cherokees would wager huge amounts on the outcome of the game: baskets, pots, clothing, blankets, weapons, horses.

Ethnologist James Mooney recorded a tale around 1900 about this game in *Myths of the Cherokee*.[1] Roughly paraphrased, it goes something like this.

A long time ago, a boy lived with his mother outside of town. He never went out and did not see anyone, because his body was covered with sores, ugly spots. He was ashamed to be seen. At last his mother told him that his father was Thunder. Thunder came down to earth from time to time in the form of a man, and when he did, he had his fun. She also told him that Thunder was the greatest of all doctors and could cure his spots. After that, she could only say that Thunder lived to the west. The boy was determined to find him, so his mother prepared him some new clothes and some trail food and sent him on his way.

He traveled far and long, and everywhere he found people, he asked them about the whereabouts of Thunder. All anyone would say was "to the west." He must have traveled across the country, clear to what is now California. He at last came to a house occupied by a man who was known as Brass. Brass lived alone with his wife in a small house. Outside the house was a gatayusti playing field. Brass was a passionate gatayusti player and gambler. He was, in fact, the inventor of the game. Brass was made of brass, and he was a shape shifter.

When the boy stopped to ask about Thunder, Brass said, "He just lives over the next hill. I hear him rumbling around all the time." The boy thanked him and started to go on his way, but Brass stopped him and insisted that he play the game with him. The boy said he had nothing to bet. Brass said, cruelly, "We could play for your pretty spots." The boy ignored the crude remark and excused himself, saying that he had to get on over to see Thunder. Reluctantly, Brass let him go after the boy promised that he would stop by on his way back home to play with him.

Word of the boy's approach had reached Thunder, and he knew that the boy claimed to be his son. "Any boy would want to be the son of Thunder," Thunder said, so he devised some tests for the boy. When the boy finally arrived, Thunder showed him a seat and told him to sit down. It was a chair covered by a blanket, but underneath the blanket, the chair was actually constructed of honey locust, with the long sharp thorns all sticking up. The boy sat down and was comfortable. Thunder asked the boy why he had come.

"I have these sores all over my body, and my mother told me to find you."

"I can fix those," Thunder said, and he told his wife to set a huge pot of water on the fire to boil. When the water had started boiling, Thunder threw in some roots. Then he picked up the boy and put him in the boiling water. He let him boil for a long time, but the boy was all right. Then Thunder told his wife to take the pot, boy and all, and throw it into the river. Thunder's wife did as she was told. When the pot with the still boiling water in it hit the river, it created an eddy. A service tree and a calico bush were growing on the bank nearby. A great cloud of steam arose and made streaks and blotches on their bark. They were the spots that had come off of the boy. When he came out of the water, he was clean.

Thunder's wife had helped the boy, and they were walking back to the house. She had taken a liking to him by this time, and she told him that there was one more test. She told him how to deal with it. When they got back to the house, Thunder said that his son needed new clothes. He gave the boy a new suit of buckskin and a belt. The boy put them on. Then Thunder opened up a box and told the boy to pick out a necklace and bracelets for himself. The boy opened the lid and found that the box was filled with writhing snakes. Remembering what Thunder's wife had told him, he plunged his hand all the way to the bottom of the box through all the snakes and grabbed hold of one. He drew out a rattlesnake, which he wrapped around his neck for a necklace. He reached in again, four more times, and each time he brought out a copperhead. These he wrapped around his wrists and ankles.

Thunder gave the boy a war club. There was one last test. "Now you have to play a ball game with your brothers," he said. The boy knew that he would have to fight for his life, and it would be one against two. The Thunder boys showed up ready to play. Both were older and stronger than the boy, but he played against them, and thunder rolled and lightning flashed with every stroke. They were the thunders, but the boy was Lightning. When Lightning grew tired, he aimed a blow at the honey locust tree in the playing field, as Thunder's wife had told him to do, and the blow was a flash of lightning. The tree was Thunder's favorite tree, and Thunder did not want to see it hurt. He quickly called an end to the game.

Then Lightning told his father about his encounter with Brass and how he had promised Brass that he would return to play him a game. Thunder knew Brass. "He'll cheat," he said, "but I'll show you how to win." Thunder produced a gourd with a hole in one end. Out of the hole dangled a string of beads. "This string of beads has no end," Thunder said. "You can bet these. Even when you win, though, he will try to cheat you. He is hard to beat, but this time he will lose every game. At last he will bet his life, but before you can collect, he will run away. When that happens, call your brothers."

Lightning went back to the home of Brass and showed him the gourd. He drew out the string of beads until it encircled the playing field and bet that. They played the game, and Lightning won. Brass wanted to play again, and again, and again. At last he had nothing left to bet. "I'll bet you my wife," he said. The boy accepted the bet and won the next game. Then Brass bet his life. The boy won again. "Just let me go inside and tell my wife what has happened," Brass said. Lightning agreed. Brass went into the house, but the house had a back door, and he ran out again. Lightning called out for his brothers, who came along bringing their pet, the Horned Green Beetle, and the four boys with the Beetle ran after Brass.

They came across an old woman making pottery beside the road. "Have you seen Brass?" they asked. She said she had not. Just then the Great Beetle flew high up into the sky and came diving back down fast. He struck the old woman on the forehead, and it rang like brass. Brass sprang up in his right shape and ran. Some of the brass had rubbed off on the Beetle. They chased Brass again, but he was awfully fast. They lost sight of him. Then they came across an old man sitting beside the road carving a stone pipe. They asked him if he had seen Brass, and he said no, but the Beetle again made a dive and struck the old man on the forehead, and again when he hit, it made a sound like striking brass. The old man turned into Brass and again ran. This time he ran to the edge of the world to the great water, and the boys caught up with him. They tied his arms and legs with grapevine and ran a long pole through his chest and pinned him to the ocean floor. They put two crows on the end of the pole to guard it, and they called the place Kogayi, meaning Crow Place.

Brass was not dead though. Sometimes the beavers, who are friends of Brass, come round to gnaw at the grapevines, but they make the pole shake, and that alerts the crows, who cry out, "Ka! Ka!," and frighten the beavers away. Brass will stay there until the end of the world, because he cannot die.

This is just about my favorite of all the old Cherokee tales. Cherokees gambled on other games, too—on the stickball game (it's mentioned in the story above), on footraces, and on less athletic games as well. Perhaps that's why I like the casinos. Gambling is in the Cherokee blood. Who knows?

So let's get back to the casinos. As I said before, they are very controversial. When they first started springing up, I heard people say, "The Mafia will get involved." I said, "Maybe, but so what? Why shouldn't Indians get some of that Mafia money?" I think there are people who just don't want to see Indians make any money. All their lives they've heard that Indians are poor, and they want to keep it that way. These misguided people are just being traditional, I suppose. But the casinos did spring up, and they are still springing up all around the country.

It all started in 1987 when the U.S. Supreme Court ruled that Indian tribes had the right to operate casinos on Indian land. Right away, the federal government got into the act. Congress passed the Indian Gaming Regulatory Act (IGRA) in 1988, requiring Indian tribes to enter into compacts with the state governments before they can operate casinos. Ordinarily states have no jurisdiction on Indian land, so it seems to me that IGRA is a major infringement on tribal governments. But we have it, so we have to live with it.

In the 1970s and early 1980s, no one in Oklahoma ever expected to see casinos, Indian or otherwise, inside the limits of this state. In a state built on graft and corruption (if you don't believe me, read Angie Debo's *And Still the Waters Run*), there are still "good" people who don't like having these palaces of sin among us. Today there are at least ninety-eight Indian casinos in the state of Oklahoma. The Cherokee Nation alone has ten. The United Keetoowah Band of Cherokee Indians in Oklahoma has one. The largest casino in the state, called RiverWind, is located in Norman and is run by the Chickasaw Nation.

Casinos have been controversial from the beginning. First of all, Indian casinos are controversial for the same reasons that any casino is controversial. There are plenty of people who just believe that gambling is wrong. It is sinful. Or it is a wasteful addiction that ruins lives and breaks up families. Perhaps it does, but then so do many other things. Drinking alcohol for instance. But the do-gooders (non-Indians and some Cherokees) seem to focus their attacks more on the Indian casinos than on non-Indian casinos. Why is that? Perhaps the country had gotten used to having a few sinful spots (Las Vegas, Reno, and so forth) and learned to live with that as long as their own neighborhoods were safe from wickedness. Let the sinners all gather in those dens of iniquity and leave the rest of us alone. But in areas where there are Indian tribes, casinos can suddenly spring up in one's own backyard. Run for cover!

Some of the other complaints about Indian casinos are that the Indian tribes' non-Indian partners are actually making more money than are the tribes. That may be true in some cases, but even so, the tribe is still making more money than it did before, and the tribe entered into an agreement with those partners with open eyes. It has also been said that small groups of people of dubious Indian identity have somehow managed to receive federal recognition as Indian tribes only to operate casinos. If that is so, then the do-gooders should be zeroing in on the Bureau of Indian Affairs for having given those groups that distinction. There have been allegations of fraud and corruption. If this is so, then the Federal Bureau of Investigation (FBI) is to blame for allowing it to go on, as it has federal criminal jurisdiction over the Indian casinos. Why is it not doing its job?

Some people say that they don't like to see Indians, who are already impoverished, losing their money in casinos. If they're already impoverished, they don't have much to lose, and they might actually win. But I believe that there are far more white people (and blacks, Mexicans, Asians, and so forth) playing in the Indian casinos than Indians. And the Indian tribes are making money—most of them for the first time ever! Where Indian tribes have been impoverished for centuries, they are now building their own health clinics and schools. Many "casino tribes" are making per capita payments to their tribal members. Tribal members are driving BMWs. Their houses now have electricity and running water. What in the world can be wrong with that?

In the final analysis, nothing bad or negative can be said about Indian casinos that cannot be said about all the other casinos in this country. So let's attack them all, or let's leave them all alone. Why single out certain casinos only because they are partly owned by Indian tribes? Why, unless you are anti-Indian?

I have also heard people say that the Indian casinos are not going to last. One of these days the government is going to put a stop to them. But consider this. Most of the casinos, if not all of them, are paying huge amounts of money into their respective state treasuries. Have you ever heard of a state voluntarily giving up a huge portion of its revenue? I think, for the first time in history, the state governments are going to become the strongest supporters of tribal sovereignty, for no other reason than that they want to hang on to that money. And even if the casinos really are not going to last, the tribes will be better off for having operated them for as long as they can.

According to recent statistics, there are about 360 Indian casinos in the United States being operated by about 220 tribes. (There are 562 federally recognized Indian tribes in the country, so obviously not all tribes have elected to run casinos.) "The largest casino in the United States, Foxwoods Casino, is owned by the Mashantucket Pequot Tribe and located in Ledyard, Connecticut." Tribal casinos in 2002 took in around $3.8 billion.[2]

Cherokee Nation Enterprises, which operates the Cherokee Nation's casinos at the request of Principal Chief Chad Smith, prepared a report on where the Cherokee casino money goes. According to that report, published as a supplement to the April 2007 issue of the *Cherokee Phoenix*, Cherokee Nation casinos in 2006 made $353 million. Operating costs were $148.7 million (41 percent). Payroll accounts for $101 million (30 percent). The state of Oklahoma received payments totaling $16.3 million (5 percent), leaving a profit of $87 million (25 percent). One hundred percent of the profit, according to the report, "is used to either create more jobs for Cherokees or to provide services for Cherokees. . . . The Cherokee Nation employs more than 6,500 people, compared with 3,000 just four years ago."

The really significant figures in the report are, first of all, the number of people employed and the amount of the payroll, and the payroll figure is the casinos' payroll, not the total Cherokee Nation payroll. And this is in an area that was described as recently as the 1970s as an economically depressed area. The second really significant figure is, of course, the $16.3 million going to the state of Oklahoma. This is money for which the state doesn't have to do a damn thing, and it can use that money any way it wants to use it.

We in tribal government and in Native American studies programs in colleges and universities across the country have talked and talked about tribal sovereignty for years. Someone finally acted on it. Federal Indian law works like this. Originally, tribes were sovereign nations. The United States came along and took away bits and pieces of that sovereignty by treaties and by federal laws. But any aspect of that original sovereignty that has not been specifically taken away still remains with the tribe. The federal government, in the U.S. Constitution, reserved the right to deal with Indian tribes to itself. The states are out of the picture. Indian tribes within a state are not a part of that state. The state has no jurisdiction on Indian land. And the federal government has no laws prohibiting gambling. Therefore, the tribes, or nations, have every right to run casinos. (As mentioned above, they do have to sign compacts with the states now, according to law, and I consider that an imposition, but Indians are living with that.)

The casinos are not only making money, big money, for the tribes, they are also often, if not usually, contributing large amounts to their respective states, and they are providing a great deal of employment to tribal members and to others as well. The casino itself, usually operating around the clock, employs a great many people. Then most casinos have at least a snack bar. The larger ones have several restaurants in them, and some have bars. Many of them also have gift shops and smoke shops. That's a bunch of jobs, and in many cases these casinos and therefore these jobs are in areas with large unemployment figures. The impact of the casinos cannot be overemphasized.

I think the Indian casinos are here to stay, and I for one am glad of it. Three cheers for the Indian casinos. I hope they are here to stay. I believe they are. They have to stay around at least long enough for Donnie Birchfield to complete his study.

Ricochet

Some of the earliest and fondest memories I have are of sitting on the front porch of my grandfather's house and listening to Grandpa tell stories of the old days in northeast Oklahoma (or Indian Territory before statehood). Grandpa—Benjamin Franklin Conley—was born in 1887 and lived through some rough times. Those times gave him lots of stories, and the story I remember the best involved Charley Wickliffe, at least peripherally.

The year was 1906. Grandpa was nineteen years old, and he had been to a dance with a full-blood Cherokee girl. (Grandpa was a mixed-blood, from a family that still has members today who claim to be "pure white.") He had given this girl a ring but was having second thoughts. The dance had lasted well into the night, and Grandpa and his girlfriend wound up walking home in the wee hours of the morning. Having a long walk yet ahead of them, they decided to stop for what was left of the night at the home of an older full-blood Cherokee woman they knew. (If Grandpa remembered the names of these women, he never used them when telling this tale.) The woman welcomed them, and they made pallets on the floor.

About the time they got settled in, they heard a ruckus outside: the sounds of horses' hooves, baying hound dogs, and men's voices. Soon a big white man with a handlebar mustache and two six-guns barged into the house. He identified himself as a deputy United States marshal named Gilstrap. He was leading a posse in search of Charley Wickliffe, and they had with them an Indian prisoner named Looney Bear. They also had two hounds.

Grandpa knew about Charley Wickliffe. He was a full-blood Cherokee who was wanted for only one crime: the killing of deputy marshals. Everywhere Charley went, his two younger brothers, John and Tom, accompanied him. In those days, Grandpa was a schoolteacher, and he had seen the three Wickliffes on several occasions as they walked past his schoolhouse at Gideon (in present-day Cherokee County, Oklahoma) wearing long yellow rain slickers and carrying Winchester rifles.

Gilstrap did not ask, he told the woman whose house he had invaded that he intended to stay the night there. Then he moved in the whole posse and the prisoner. Soon the floor was covered with pallets, and everyone was asleep and snoring. Well, almost everyone. Grandpa and his girlfriend were still awake, and they were having an argument. He wanted his ring back, and she wouldn't give it up. He tried to take it away from her, and she took a tumble, landing on Gilstrap. The deputy awoke and came to his feet all at once, a gun in each hand. He arrested them all and said he'd take them all in the next morning. But after a good night's sleep, he apparently forgot about the arrest.

He got his posse ready to move after breakfast, but before leaving the house, he asked its owner where he could find Charley Wickliffe. She said she didn't know, and he slapped her around a bit. Then she said, "I don't know where Charley is, but I hope you find him, 'cause when you do, he's going to shoot you right between the eyes." Gilstrap laughed and left, and later Grandpa heard the news. Gilstrap's posse had been ambushed, and Gilstrap had been killed by one bullet right between the eyes. The dogs had been killed too, and their bodies tossed on top of Gilstrap's.

I thought it was a great story. I still do. And I tried two or three times over the years to write it up and get it into print, but never with any success. Finally I wrote it as fiction. I called the story "Wickliffe," even though Charley never actually appears in the story, and it was published in my collection, *The Witch of Goingsnake and Other Stories*. But getting back to my grandpa's tale—the nonfiction story—I've never heard or read anything from anyone else about Gilstrap's stopover for the night and the Cherokee woman's prediction (if that's what it was) of the manner of his death. In fact, I've read about Charley Wickliffe only once. "Manhunt in the

Spavinaws" by Howard Newberry appeared in *Frontier Times* in 1967. Newberry did not mention the stopover.

In 1988, shortly after my wife and I returned to Tahlequah, Oklahoma, the capital city of the Cherokee Nation, I was visiting with Cecil Dick, a highly respected Cherokee artist and old-timer. We sat together in his small studio on Muskogee Avenue sharing a bottle of peach brandy and swapping tales about outlaws.

"Do you know about Charley Wickliffe?" he asked me.

I took a slug out of the pint bottle and handed it back to Cecil.

"Yeah," I said. "I know about him."

"Let me tell you a story about Charley Wickliffe," he said. "Andy Dick was in the posse that went after him."

"Gilstrap's posse?" I asked.

"Yeah," he said. "Yeah. That one. The time they killed Gilstrap, you know. And you know what Andy Dick told me about that? He said the bullet that killed Gilstrap, the bullet that hit him right between the eyes, was a ricochet."

Stand Watie and the Treaty of 1866

Let us consider Stand Watie. He was a hell of a man. He is one of the most revered and at the same time one of the most hated men in Cherokee history. He is remembered largely because he was the only American Indian general in the Confederate army and was the last Confederate general to surrender. That's quite a legacy. But let's start out considering the rest of his life, his early life, his life before the Civil War.

He was born on December 12, 1806, at Oothcaloga, near New Echota in the Cherokee Nation, in what is now Cass County, Georgia, to Oowatie (the Ancient One) and Susanna Reese. Oowatie was a full-blood Cherokee. His wife was half Cherokee and half white. Upon their conversion to Christianity, they took the "Christian" names of Christian David Watie and Susanna Charity Watie. Their first son was known as Buck Watie. Their second son was given the Cherokee name of Degataga (Mooney translates the name as "two persons standing together and so closely united in sympathy as to form but one human body") and the "Christian" name of Isaac S. Watie.[1] Somewhere along the line, Degataga, or Isaac Watie, translated his Cherokee name into English and took a much shortened version of it for his first name to become known as Stand Watie. His older brother, upon finishing school at the Moravian Mission School at Springplace, was sent to school at Cornwall, Connecticut. His benefactor was a man named Elias Boudinot, so Buck, to honor the man, took his name.

So now we have two full brothers, one named Stand Watie and the other Elias Boudinot. Both men had children and have descendants to this day. Stand Watie's descendants are named Watie, and Elias Boudinot's descendants are named Boudinot. There were other Watie children. Elias and Stand next had a brother named Thomas Black; then four sisters, Nancy, Mary Ann, Elizabeth, and Susan; and then two more brothers, John Alexander and Charles Edwin.

In 1813, the Creek War, also known as the Red Stick War, broke out, and many Cherokees joined General Andrew Jackson's army to fight against the Red Stick Creeks. Oowatie, or David Watie, was one of them. Stand was only seven years old. David was made a captain in the Cherokee regiment, which was commanded by the Ridge (according to Mooney, a name formed by the translation of a Cherokee name, Guhnuhndalegi, "One Who Follows the Ridge," shortened after translation). The Ridge was David Watie's older brother. For his service in the war, he was named a major and thereafter took that rank as his first name. He became known as Major Ridge.

Unlike his older brother, Elias Boudinot, Stand Watie did not go to school beyond the Moravian Mission School. When his education was finished there, he went to work on his father's farm. He had been baptized and joined the church while a student. Elias returned from Connecticut with a white wife, Harriet Ruggles Boudinot. The Cherokee Nation had gone into a period of purposeful assimilation, imitating the ways of the whites in an effort to avoid removal. The Ridge and Watie families were important in this movement. They were prosperous farmers and slave owners. In addition, David Watie operated a ferry.

In 1828, the year following the adoption of the first Cherokee constitution, Stand Watie was appointed clerk of the Cherokee Nation Supreme Court. He was twenty-two years old. Sometime during the following years, he married three times, first to Elizabeth Fields, who died. His next marriage was to Isabel Hicks. Her fate is unknown. His third was to Eleanor Looney. Nothing more is known of Eleanor. Stand Watie apparently had no children as a result of these three marriages.

When Andrew Jackson was inaugurated as president of the United States in 1829, pressure on the Cherokees for their removal to the West increased. Cherokee resistance increased accordingly, with leaders of that movement being Principal Chief John Ross, the Ridges, and the Waties. Elias Boudinot became the first editor of the *Cherokee Phoenix*, the first Indian newspaper and a bilingual publication. In 1834, Stand Watie became interpreter for the Cherokee Agency. But when Jackson refused to enforce the U.S. Supreme Court's ruling that supported the Cherokee position against removal, the Ridges and Waties gave up. They figured they had taken the fight as far as it could go and decided therefore that the best course of action was to go ahead and move west. Chief John Ross disagreed, and thereafter they and Ross became bitter enemies.

On December 29, 1835, Major Ridge, his son John Ridge, Stand Watie, Elias Boudinot, and eighteen other Cherokees signed the Treaty of New Echota, a treaty of complete removal of the Cherokees to lands west of the Mississippi River. Although they were not official representatives of the Cherokee Nation, the U.S. government looked upon the document as a legally binding treaty. The signers became known as the Treaty Party. For his part in securing the treaty, Stand Watie was paid $1,419. In June 1836, Stand Watie bought three slaves for $1,300. He was then paid $2,392 for the improvements he had made to the land he was losing, and his wife (the second) received $3,095. Stand Watie also received $1,427 removal expenses. His wife received $1,665. Under other provisions of the treaty, he received $20 and $1,328.46, and his wife $812. While Chief Ross and the majority of the Cherokees continued to resist removal, the Treaty Party moved west to join the Western Cherokees, Cherokees who had voluntarily moved west beginning in 1794, first to Missouri, then in 1811 into Arkansas.

Stand Watie selected a spot for his new home slightly northwest of Southwest City, Missouri. He busied himself establishing a new home. In the years since his appointment as clerk of the Cherokee Nation Supreme Court, Watie had earned the right to practice law in the Cherokee Nation. He had plenty of money. He and his wife together had secured over $12,000, a considerable sum in those days, and it's safe to assume that he already had some socked away.

When the majority of Cherokees were forcibly removed from the East in 1838–39, more than 4,000 died. There had been much suffering over the Trail of Tears. They arrived in the West embittered and angry. The focus of that anger became the treaty signers, or the Treaty Party. On June 22, 1839, four groups of conspirators went off in different directions. One group of twenty-five men went to the home of John Ridge. Three of the men broke into Ridge's house. One fired a pistol at Ridge, who was lying in bed, ill, but the pistol misfired. The three men dragged Ridge outside, where each of the twenty-five men plunged a knife into him as his wife and young son watched in horror. Then the men tossed his body into the air, and in turn, each man stomped on it.

At about the same time, a second band of around thirty men approached a building site where Elias Boudinot was helping with the construction. They hid in some nearby trees. Four of them approached Boudinot, asking for medicine for sick members of their families. He agreed to help them and went walking down the path with them. As they passed the trees where the remaining men were hidden, the men burst out and stabbed him with knives and hacked him with hatchets. As his wife and others came rushing to his aid, the killers fled. One witness to the killing jumped on the Reverend Sam Worcester's horse and hurried away toward Stand Watie's store.

Major Ridge was riding a lone trail in Arkansas when he was shot dead from his horse's back by men lying in ambush.

When the man who had carried the warning to Stand Watie arrived at Watie's store, he found the place crowded with would-be killers, apparently awaiting the right moment to make their attack. The messenger pretended to want to buy some sugar and pulled Watie aside, where he gave him the news. Watie went out the back door and mounted Worcester's horse, which had been left there for him. He raced to the site where his brother's body lay. He found a crowd gathered there, which included many men from the Ross Party, the opposition party. Ignoring the danger, he looked at Boudinot's body, then turned to the crowd and said aloud, "I will give $10,000 for the names of the men that did this." He got no response.

These killings brought about more killings, and they in turn brought even more, until the Cherokee Nation was practically embroiled in a civil war. Stand Watie gathered about fifteen men around him and for a time searched for the killers, but to no avail. Chief Ross, in the meantime, complained to General Matthew Arbuckle of the U.S. Army stationed at Fort Gibson that Watie had threatened his life. Ross had many men gathered around his home at Park Hill. Stand Watie and his followers fled to Fort Gibson for safety and the protection of the U.S. Army. On July 25, 1839, a meeting was held at which the Cherokee Nation and the Western Cherokees were reunited. Killers from both parties were granted amnesty. Stand Watie, as de facto leader of the Treaty Party, refused to recognize Ross as chief of all the Cherokees. He held meetings of the Treaty Party and passed resolutions against Ross and his actions. He protested to the U.S. government. He even led a delegation of Cherokees, members of the Treaty Party and members of the old Western Cherokee band, to Washington, D.C., to propose that the U.S. government recognize two separate Cherokee nations because, he said, the two groups could never live in peace under one government. None of his efforts were rewarded.

In 1840, Archilla Smith, a treaty signer, was arrested by the Cherokee Nation and put on trial for murder. Stand Watie was his defense attorney. John Howard Payne, internationally known playwright and actor who was visiting at the home of Chief Ross, attended the trial and recorded it. Payne's little book is still kept in print by the University of Oklahoma Press as *Indian Justice: A Cherokee Murder Trial at Tahlequah in 1840*. Stand Watie, however, lost the case, and Smith was hanged, the first man to be hanged by the Cherokee Nation in its new home in the West. Many believed at the time, and many still believe, that the trial was a put-up deal, and that Archilla Smith was simply another treaty signer killed by the Ross Party.

On May 14, 1842, Stand Watie, his brother John, and James P. Miller were traveling from Watie's home at Honey Creek to Van Buren, Arkansas. They had gone about three miles into Arkansas and stopped at a store. James Foreman, accused of being one of the killers of Major Ridge, was there with several of his friends. Foreman tried to borrow a horse to send a man for his guns. When asked why he wanted them, he gestured toward Stand Watie. He was refused the loan of the horse.

Stand Watie had ordered a drink, and Foreman picked it up and drank it. He handed the glass back to Watie with the comment, "Here is wishing that you may live forever." Stand Watie said, "Jim, I suppose I can drink with you, but I understood a few days since that you were going to kill me." Foreman replied, "Say yourself." Stand Watie threw his glass to the floor. Foreman produced a whip and began to beat Watie with it. Foreman's uncle, attempting to get behind Watie, fell through the door. Foreman followed him outside. He picked up a board. Stand Watie burst through the door with a knife in his hand and stabbed Foreman. Foreman backed off and said, "You haven't done it yet." Watie drew his pistol and fired a shot at Foreman. Foreman was wounded but still alive. He ran about 150 yards and fell through a gap in a fence, where he finally died.

Watie surrendered himself to Arkansas authorities, had the trial postponed, and was released on bail. In September, he was married, for the fourth time, to Sarah Caroline Bell. When the trial finally took place in December, Watie was acquitted on the grounds of self-defense.

Allow me to digress a bit. Here is what I think is significant about this episode. I started this essay by saying, "Let us consider. . . ." All right. Let us consider that the life of Stand Watie, up until this point, had been very calm for a life passed during such a tumultuous period. What had he been? A businessman, a bureaucrat, and a politician. Even when his uncle, his cousin, and his brother had been cruelly killed, and his own life threatened, and when he had made so bold a statement over the bloody body of his brother, what had he done? Nothing! In three years, he had done nothing in retaliation. Nothing other than have his Treaty Party pass resolutions and make protests to the federal government against John Ross. And then when he killed James Foreman, he had done so not in retaliation but only in self-defense. He had remained awfully calm for a man we in later years consider to have been a man of action.

Even when John Rollin Ridge, the son of John Ridge who as a youngster had witnessed his father's killing, wrote his uncle Stand letters from Missouri and later from California urging him to take the lead in organizing some kind of action against John Ross and his government, Watie put him off, advising him to remain calm and patient.

Things went on like this for several more years. In 1844, Watie and some other members of the Treaty Party took a petition to Washington in which they said, among other things, that if they were to die at the hands of assassins, they would "perish like men." More bold talk. Still no action. However, killings continued on both sides. In 1843, a relative period of calm ensued after the federal government threatened to send an army to enforce the peace. But violence erupted again in 1845, due in large part to the actions of the Starr family.

That year, James Starr, a treaty signer who had so far escaped retaliation, was killed at his home by a large group of men. Thomas, Stand Watie's younger brother, was killed five days later when several men stopped by his house and found him in bed. He was slain by hatchet and knife. Stand Watie's reaction? With sixty followers, he gathered at Old Fort Wayne and began hoarding guns and ammunition. He vowed to avenge his brother's death. He appealed to the federal government for help.

On the other hand, the Starrs, under the leadership of Tom Starr, began retaliating. It is probably an exaggeration, but it has been said that Tom Starr killed one hundred men in retaliation for his father's killing. He was so feared that eventually the Cherokee Nation forgave his many sins and made peace with him. He died peacefully, an old man. History's vengeance on Tom Starr is that his worthless son Sam married a white woman from Missouri named Myra Belle Shirley, who became famous as Belle Starr. Her name has practically eclipsed that of the rest of the Starrs.

While the Starrs were engaged in mass destruction, Stand Watie urged his own men to "abstain from excesses, and to *suffer wrong* rather than be the aggressors" (my emphasis). He continued to press the federal government for monies due Treaty Party members from the Removal Treaty, for protection against Chief Ross, for an investigation into the doings of the Ross government, and for a separate Cherokee Nation. A fence was erected around Old Fort Wayne. The fort was renamed Fort Watie. During all this mess, Stand Watie and Caroline Bell Watie had their first son, named Saladin.

In 1846, the federal government finally negotiated a treaty that was signed by all three factions of the Cherokee Nation: the Cherokee Nation (the Ross faction), the Treaty Party, and the Western Cherokees. Everyone seemed to be satisfied, and the old differences seemed to be resolved. Peace had come at last. Watie returned to his farm on Honey Creek, apparently resolved to lead a private life and spend time with his family. He was called on, however, to represent the interests of the Treaty Party from time to time. In 1849, Solon Watica, his second son, was born, and Stand Watie was once again serving as clerk of the Cherokee Nation Supreme Court. John Rollin Ridge continued to plague him with letters calling for some sort of action against Ross. But Stand Watie seemed to be satisfied.

In 1851, his third son, Cumiskey, was born, followed in 1852 by his first daughter, Ninnie Josephine. In 1853, he was elected to the Cherokee National Council from Delaware District. That same year, he began his legal practice. He was reelected in 1855 and served as Speaker. Several slave-holding Cherokees had been expelled from mission churches, and the issue of abolitionist efforts became a major one. Stand Watie was party to a resolution that said, in part, "Cherokee people, are and have been for many years a Slave holding People," and "the Constitution . . . and laws of the Cherokee Nation recognized the institution of Slavery." In 1857, Stand Watie was reelected to the National Council and retained his position as Speaker. His fifth child, Charlotte Jacqueline, was born that year.

Stand Watie was operating a prosperous steam sawmill and lumber business, and a dry goods and general merchandise store. He was acquiring a fair amount of wealth. So how do we interpret his actions? Here is Stand Watie, avowed enemy of the John Ross government, serving in that very government. How did John Rollin Ridge take this information? At the very least, he had to have been disappointed. He had been urging Stand Watie to lead an armed rebellion against John Ross. What happened to Stand Watie's vows of revenge for the deaths of his two brothers? He seems to have forgotten them. He is wealthy. He is raising a family. He is comfortable. Some might call him selfish. He would like to avenge his brothers, but not enough to jeopardize his own comforts.

Some might say that his actions were cowardly. He had as many as sixty men around him, but he told them to do nothing. They were bodyguards. But judging from his later actions, during the Civil War, we know that Stand Watie was no coward. Looking backward, with the full knowledge of his life, it is difficult to fathom why Stand Watie's actions during the 1840s and 1850s were not more like those of Tom Starr. We would expect them to be. But they were not. During these years, Watie remained the businessman, the bureaucrat, the politician. Nominally, at least, he was a Christian. Could that explain his behavior? Perhaps he needed the comfort of a legitimate force behind his actions, the security of a government, the cause of a just war. Well, it was coming.

By the late 1850s, the entire United States was divided, largely over the issue of slavery. The Cherokee Nation was no different. Stand Watie and his followers, the Treaty Party, urged the Cherokee Nation to align itself with the South. They became known as the Knights of the Golden Circle. John Ross did his best to keep the Cherokee Nation neutral, to stay out of it. His followers, many of them, either formed or revived an ancient Cherokee society known as the Keetoowahs, and because they used identifying pins under their coat lapels, they became known as the "Pins" or Pin Indians.

Leaders of the Confederate states began courting the Cherokees. Chief Ross adamantly refused to be persuaded. In 1861, two men from Arkansas approached Stand Watie and urged him to help them protect the region from abolitionism. They assured him that if he did so, the rights of the Cherokee Nation would be ensured. In July 1861, Stand Watie was commissioned a colonel in the Army of the Confederacy. Chief Ross, afraid that a Cherokee civil war might be about to erupt, signed a treaty with the Confederacy. In July 1862, just about a year later, John Ross was captured by an invading Union force. Many of Chief Ross's "Confederate Cherokees" had already deserted to the Union side. Many had refused to fight against Union soldiers. Ross went to Washington and repudiated the treaty with the Confederacy, claiming that he had signed it under coercion. The Cherokee Nation was left in the hands of Stand Watie.

A meeting was called of the Confederate Cherokees, and Stand Watie was elected chief. The Pins continued to resist, even though their chief was sitting out the war in Washington, D.C., and Pennsylvania. I am not going to take up time or space here to go over once again the accomplishments of Stand Watie during the Civil War. They have been amply covered in several books and dozens of articles in magazines and journals. If you've missed them and you're interested, you can look especially for *Stand Watie and the Agony of the Cherokee Nation* by Kenny A. Franks, and *General Stand Watie's Confederate Indians* by Frank Cunningham. Suffice it here to say that Watie was highly praised by a number of Confederate generals and politicians and has been highly thought of by later historians. General Robert E. Lee surrendered on April 9, 1865, effectively ending the war. Stand Watie did not surrender until June 23, the last Confederate general to do so. He signed his letter of surrender, "Stand Watie, Principal Chief of the Cherokee Nation."

For the next year, Watie was busy with the Southern delegation of Cherokees trying to work out solutions to the problems of the two Cherokee factions. Once again, he was telling the federal government that the two could not live together in peace. He was urging the establishment of two separate Cherokee nations. John Ross died in 1866. Watie was sixty years old. His fortune had been wasted away during the war. He was tired, and his old rival was dead. He went home, leaving the fight to others younger than himself. He needed to rebuild. During the next five years, his fortunes rose and fell. His farm did well, and then not so well. He joined with his nephew Elias C. Boudinot to form the Cherokee Tobacco Company. Things looked good until the federal government interfered. Worst of all, he lost two of his sons, Saladin and Watica. Stand Watie died on September 9, 1871, at his home on Honey Creek. He was sixty-five years old. Let us now praise him, or let us curse him, or both.

I should say here that the old rift in the Cherokee Nation is still very much with us. You have to remember that the Confederate Cherokees were basically the old Treaty Party. The feud could almost be said to have been between the Ross Party and the Treaty Party, or between John Ross and Stand Watie (once the other leaders of the Treaty Party were dead). The parties changed names over the years. But the feud never ended.

At an art show at the Five Civilized Tribes Museum just a few years ago, Cherokee artist Murv Jacob had a painting on display that was called "The Assassination of Elias Boudinot." An older Cherokee woman walked up to Murv and said, "It was not an assassination. It was an execution." The difference, of course, is that an execution is a legal action. She was adamant about it. She was a John Ross supporter all these years after his death.

When my Cherokee Nation history was in the process of being published, a Cherokee I did not know, living in Oklahoma City, I think, called me and wanted to know if I was going to repeat the same lies about Chief Ross that had been told before. He was a Southern Rights Cherokee for sure.

So much that is felt about Stand Watie today is based on historical prejudices. Those who sympathize with Chief John Ross, of course, have nothing good to say about Stand Watie. And there are those Southern sympathizers who know little or nothing about Cherokee history but praise Watie to high heaven because he was a Confederate, and not just any Confederate, but an American Indian Confederate who was the last Confederate general to surrender. They drive around with Confederate flag decals on their car windows.

Now, I am not a mindless supporter of Chief John Ross. He used some pretty damned devious methods himself to achieve his ends. So I'm not going to say that Ross was the savior of the Cherokee Nation. I am going to say, while in the safety of my study at home, outside of the Cherokee Nation's boundaries, that Stand Watie, love him or hate him, did more damage to the Cherokee Nation than any other Cherokee in history. What? Why? How?

We don't have to detail the damage done to the Cherokee Nation during the Civil War. We don't have to say that if Chief

Ross had been let alone to keep the Cherokee Nation neutral, all of those Cherokees killed during the war would have had longer lives, the widows and orphans left at the end of the war would have still had husbands and fathers, the houses and businesses burned during the war would have still been standing after the war, the Cherokee Nation would not have felt the necessity of building a Cherokee insane asylum and a Cherokee orphanage. It's all very real, but we don't have to go into all that.

All we have to do is take a good look at the Treaty of 1866, the so-called Reconstruction Treaty. If Stand Watie had not joined the Confederacy, if John Ross had been allowed to keep the Cherokee Nation neutral, there would have been no excuse for this treaty. So I believe that it is fair to blame this treaty on Stand Watie. It was a worse treaty for the Cherokee Nation, I believe, than was the one for which his relatives were killed in 1839. Let's take a look at it.

Article 4 of the treaty reads:

> All the Cherokees and freed persons who were formerly slaves to any Cherokee, and all free negroes not having been such slaves, who resided in the Cherokee Nation prior to June first, eighteen hundred and sixty-one, who may within two years elect not to reside northeast of the Arkansas River and Southeast of Grand River, shall have the right to settle in and occupy the Canadian district southwest of the Arkansas River . . . [which will] include a quantity of land equal to one hundred and sixty acres for each person who may so elect to reside in the territory above described.

They are giving away Cherokee Nation land. Did they do that to any of the Southern states involved in the Civil War? I think not.

Article 5 stated that

> the inhabitants electing to reside in the district described in the preceding article shall have the right to elect all their local officers and judges, and the number of delegates to which by their numbers they may be entitled in any general council to be established in the Indian Territory under the

provisions of this treaty, as stated in Article XII, and to control all their local affairs, and to establish all necessary police regulations and rules for the administration of justice in said district, not inconsistent with the constitution of the Cherokee Nation or the laws of the United States: *Provided*, the Cherokees residing in such district shall enjoy all the rights and privileges of other Cherokees who may elect to settle in said district as hereinbefore provided, and shall hold the same rights and privileges and be subject to the same liabilities as those who elect to settle in said district under the provisions of this treaty; *Provided also*, That if any such police regulations or rules be adopted which, in the opinion of the President, bear oppressively on any citizen of the nation, he may suspend the same. And all rules or regulations in said district, or in any other district of the nation, discriminating against the citizens of other districts, are prohibited, and shall be void.

It sounds to me like all former black slaves of Cherokees and any black people who were not slaves but were living in the Cherokee Nation were given the right to 160 acres in the Cherokee Nation. Further, they were given voting rights. The word "citizen" is never mentioned, but everything else sounds like citizenship rights. Further, and this could slip by many readers, this article presumes that the president of the United States has certain powers over the Cherokee Nation that, I believe, had never been presumed before.

Article 6 gave the inhabitants of said district the right to representation in the Cherokee National Council. It further asserted the power of the president over the laws of the Cherokee Nation.

Article 7 created a U.S. court in Indian Territory, and gave that court jurisdiction over any case involving a resident of the district discussed in the preceding articles.

Article 9 stated that since the Cherokee Nation had abolished slavery, never again will slavery be allowed in the Cherokee Nation, and further that "all freedmen who have been liberated . . . , as well as all free colored persons who were in the country at the commencement of the rebellion, and are now residents therein, or who may return within six months, and their descendants, shall have all the rights of native Cherokees." This article is still causing problems in the Cherokee Nation today. It comes very close to making former slaves and other blacks citizens of the Cherokee Nation. Some black descendants of those people are agitating today for citizenship rights in the Cherokee Nation. The Cherokee Nation is resisting those efforts. Some people say that the Cherokee Nation is racist. Others say that the Cherokee Nation is merely trying to maintain a Cherokee blood basis for Cherokee citizenship. The issue has not been resolved at this writing.

Article 11 gave the U.S. government the right to bestow upon any company railroad right-of-way through the Cherokee Nation. This was an issue that Chief John Ross had fought against for years, reasoning that the railroad would bring all kinds of people, many of them undesirable, into the Cherokee Nation. He was right, of course—it did.

Article 12 in effect established Indian Territory, that is, it established the lands of the so-called Five Civilized Tribes into a formal territory of the United States, a first step toward statehood.

Article 13 gave the U.S. government the authority to establish courts within the Indian Territory. These courts would have jurisdiction over all cases that did not involve only members of the Indian nations.

Article 14 gave any missionary organization that had been given the right to occupy land in the Indian Territory the right to keep its land.

Article 15 gave the U.S. government the right to settle any "civilized" Indians within the Cherokee country.

Article 17 took some land away from the Cherokee Nation. Again, this did not happen to any of the rebelling Southern states.

Article 20 said that whenever the Cherokee National Council shall request it, the Cherokee lands would be surveyed and allotted. This was an ominous article, and of course allotment came about.

Article 23 gave the U.S. government control over the Cherokee Nation funds.

Article 26 was a repeat of many treaty articles throughout history and is almost ludicrous in its repetition and in the fact that it has always been ignored. It guaranteed "to the people of the Cherokee Nation the quiet and peaceable possession of their country and protection against domestic feuds and insurrections and against hostilities of other tribes. They shall also be protected against interruptions or intrusion from all unauthorized citizens of the United States who may attempt to settle on their lands."

This article, of course, was totally ignored by the United States. It is ludicrous because most of the rest of the treaty is obviously aimed at the slow destruction of the Cherokee Nation.

Article 27 gave the U.S. government the right to establish military posts within the boundaries of the Cherokee Nation.

Any careful reading of this treaty shows that the intent of the U.S. government is the final destruction of the Cherokee Nation. Without the approval of the Cherokee Nation, the railroad is going through. Cherokee courts are deprived of some of their powers, and U.S. courts are established inside the Cherokee Nation. Persons who are not Cherokee are made Cherokee citizens. U.S. military posts are established inside the Cherokee Nation. The Cherokee Nation is made part of a formal U.S. territory. The president of the United States is given the authority to render Cherokee laws that he disapproves of null and void. The U.S. government takes control of Cherokee funds. Cherokee land is taken. And allotment of Cherokee land is mentioned.

It is a devastating treaty. In my opinion, it is the worst treaty ever forced on the Cherokee Nation. It had the farthest-reaching effects, some of which are still tormenting the Cherokee Nation today. It very nearly caused the end of the Cherokee Nation. It paved the way for other treaties and for acts of Congress that caused much pain and suffering to many Cherokee people. And it would never have been signed, it would never have been drawn up, had not Stand Watie joined the Confederate army. Thank-you for that, Stand Watie. From time to time, I wonder if Stand Watie realized, after the signing of the treaty, just what his actions had accomplished. I wonder if he knew what his legacy would be. I wonder if he gave a damn.

Cherokee Wannabes

A favorite topic of conversation among many Cherokees these days is the large number of Cherokee Wannabes out there everywhere. (For the uninformed, Cherokee Wannabes are people who "want to be" Cherokees.) Every Indian tribe has some Wannabes. Apparently the number of casinos, especially those owned by tribes that make per capita payments, has dramatically increased the number of people wanting to be Indian or claiming to be Indian. That could be true in North Carolina, where the Eastern Band of Cherokees is paying out something like $6,000 twice a year to every tribal member. I should have said "to every citizen," but folks in general are just not used to the language of tribal sovereignty. Even strong spokespersons for tribal sovereignty still use some of the old misleading language. They talk about "tribal" sovereignty. "Tribe" does not have the same connotation as does "nation," although that is exactly what "sovereignty" implies. Indian tribes are nations. Members of Indian tribes are citizens of nations. And these citizens are men, women, and children, not braves or warriors, squaws, and papooses. Language is a powerful persuader, and we need to be careful with it.

But the Cherokee Nation in Oklahoma does not make per capita payments. Current principal chief Chad Smith has said that will happen "over my dead body." Chief Smith is a Republican and a lawyer who believes that people should lift themselves up by their bootstraps and not depend on social programs or handouts for help. So with no per caps, why do people want to become citizens of the Cherokee Nation? There are a bunch of people. What's in it for them?

For starters, let's consider the most organized of these people, the various Cherokee "tribes" around the country. In a book called *Cherokee Proud*, Tony Mack McClure has identified more than 250 such Cherokee "tribes." One of these groups has even gone to Mexico and miraculously obtained recognition from the state of Coahuilla. They call themselves the Mexican Cherokee Nation (or the Cherokee Nation of Mexico). There are state-recognized Cherokee tribes in the United States as well—in Georgia and a few other states—but most of these 250 groups are strictly self-identified.

They have chiefs and councils that are sometimes elected. They have interesting-sounding names. The members of these tribes (I did not say "citizens" because these groups cannot be said to have sovereignty) often give themselves or each other Indian-sounding names, names that sound Cherokee to them. I once met a Princess Running Path from Pennsylvania. She was wearing what appeared to me to be a dime store Indian dress. I was polite to her because she approached me excitedly, saying she had never met a "real live author." I thought she might buy some books. When she finally left, she said that she would check her library as soon as she got home.

These groups more often than not have their own, usually strange versions of Cherokee culture. They perform ceremonies that "real Cherokees" have never seen or heard of. They are conscious of their lack of status with the federal government, with any state government, or with any officially recognized Cherokee nation. There are three of these federally recognized Cherokee nations: the Cherokee Nation, in Oklahoma; the United Keetoowah Band of Cherokee Indians, also in Oklahoma; and the Eastern Band of Cherokees, in North Carolina. Probably embarrassed by the fact that none of these governments recognizes them, members of the self-identified Cherokee tribes will often say something like, "The federal government doesn't recognize us, and we don't recognize it."

Often they seem to have invented elaborate histories for themselves, explaining how they happen to be in Pennsylvania, or Delaware, or New York. The groups in Arkansas and Missouri have an easier time creating their history because Cherokees at least did go through those areas and even stopped over for a few years. So much for these groups. Just remember, there are at least 250 of them!

An incredibly large number of individuals say they are Cherokee but can't prove it. Often they say their ancestors dropped out along the Trail of Tears. They say that in Grandma's day, it was not popular, or it was not safe, to say that one was Cherokee, so "they passed." If they look like white people, which most of them do, they will always emphasize that Grandma was dark and had black hair and high cheekbones. Often they will name a real historical Cherokee as their ancestor, and more often than not it will be Nancy Ward. Cherokees meet these other Cherokees almost every day.

My friend Richard King, an Assiniboine from Montana, told me that he met a young black man once who claimed to be Cherokee. "I was born in a tepee," he said, "and look, I ain't got no hair on my legs." I met a white man once who told me that he was one-third Cherokee. He could not explain the mathematics. But then, we were both drunk at the time.

So what is the result of these meetings? How do the "real Cherokees" react to all of this? The most noticeable result is that some today call all of these people "Wannabes." They are people who want to be Cherokee. I know one Cherokee who can turn any conversation or discussion into a discussion of Wannabes. His mental gymnastics are incredible. He can be in a meeting in which the topic is the Cherokee casino, or the Johnson O'Malley Program, or the Repatriation Act, or anything else, and he will come out with some statement about Wannabes. It's a major preoccupation with him. It is his main, sometimes I think his only, topic of conversation.

I once had a conversation with a Cherokee, a citizen of the Cherokee Nation, who said that no one could be called Cherokee unless he or she was in possession of a tribal membership card and a Certificate of Degree of Indian Blood (CDIB). I asked him if that meant that if he and his wife should have a new infant, that the infant would not be Cherokee until they had gone to the Cherokee Nation's registration office and done all the necessary paperwork. He said, yes, that was true. There are others who feel the same way. Why?

For one thing, when people have been put down for so many generations, and then all of a sudden their oppressors begin wanting to be a part of them, they naturally resent it, especially when those people come from outside their communities. But it's more than that. There's a lot of history involved.

The first Cherokee Wannabe in history was possibly Major John Norton. Norton claimed to have been born of a Scottish father and a Cherokee mother. He was probably born in Scotland around 1760. He arrived in Canada with the British army but soon left the army to become a schoolteacher among the Mohawks. He learned their culture so well, he was eventually adopted as a nephew by Chief Joseph Brant. When Brant died in 1807, Norton is said to have become chief. He led the Mohawks during the War of 1812 for two years, fighting alongside British regulars. After the war, he received a pension for being in the British army and settled down to a peaceful life on the Grand River Reservation with a wife. Accused of killing a man in a duel in 1823, he left the reservation. Back in Britain, he wrote his journals, giving valuable information on the War of 1812 and on Mohawk culture. He apparently returned to the Mohawk reservation sometime before 1826, because he is said to have left again that year in the company of a young Cherokee cousin. He briefly visited Cherokee country, and then left again, winding up in California, where, according to his cousin, he died around 1831.

Some historians have found fault with Norton's story. They don't believe that he was Cherokee. They also don't find the dates given to be plausible. If they are right, Norton was the first Cherokee Wannabe. But then, they might not be right. Norton could as easily have been the first misplaced Cherokee who has been thus accused. Either way, Norton, although a fascinating historical personality, is not that well known today and probably does not have much to do with current attitudes.

The first major event in Cherokee history that involves Wannabes (although the word was not in use then) probably occurred when the Dawes Commission went to work in the Cherokee

Nation in preparation for Oklahoma statehood. The job of the Dawes Commission was to enroll all Cherokees (in what later became Oklahoma) in order to assign them each an allotment of land. The idea was to make all Cherokees private land-owning citizens of the United States and the new state of Oklahoma, and to dissolve the Cherokee Nation. Many white people came into the Cherokee Nation, claiming Cherokee blood in order to acquire a share of the Cherokee land. These were the first Wannabes that anyone remembers. They wanted to be Cherokees for personal profit. These were the ones who most likely created the resentful attitude that many Cherokees have toward anyone who appears to be white and claims to be Cherokee. And they were a despicable bunch (although probably less despicable than those who married Cherokee women just to get some Cherokee land).

But land is no longer an issue in claiming Cherokee blood. So we are right back where we started, and let's consider all of these people who are now claiming to be Cherokee but have no proof. Now I will probably aggravate some Cherokees, but I tend to believe that most of those people really believe they are Cherokee. I would go even further and say that most of them probably are Cherokee. Let's examine the history again.

If Major John Norton really did have a Cherokee mother, a Cherokee woman who married a British army officer and went back to Scotland with him, there could easily have been others like him. Some of them may not have claimed their Cherokee blood, as did Norton. Somewhere along the line, someone may have said to a child in that family, "Oh, by the way, you have Cherokee blood in you." That's a long shot, but it is a possibility.

An even stronger possibility comes from the Trail of Tears. I already mentioned that many of these people will say they had an ancestor who dropped off along the trail. That is a very real possibility. The journals kept along the trail note the fact that people did drop off. Some of the leaders of the groups kept journals in which they recorded the number of deaths, the number of births, and the number of runaways from the previous day or night. One such journal gives numbers of runaways every single day along the way. There were thirteen contingents or waves of immigrants on the trail. If the other waves had a similar number of escapees, then the number was large indeed. And how many generations have passed since then? Depending on where these people dropped off and where they went after that, they could easily have descendants in all parts of the United States.

There are certainly Cherokee claimants in all parts of the United States. My wife and I travel a great deal, and everywhere we go, we meet someone who tells us that he or she is Cherokee. In most of these places, I am speaking or teaching a workshop or just having a book signing. My wife sells my books and sometimes sells products made by a variety of Cherokee artists. These people who claim to be Cherokee are often, almost always, good customers. We have had people speak to us about their Cherokee background and then break down into tears. It is obviously something very close to their hearts. It means a great deal to them. One might even say that it seems to mean everything.

I know some "undocumented Cherokees" in California who are very much involved in Cherokee Nation politics—as far as they can be. They sponsor meetings of Cherokees in Los Angeles. They have gone so far as to host candidates for principal chief when those candidates have gone to California to stump for votes. (The Cherokee Nation has absentee voting, and large numbers of citizens live in California.) Some travel to Oklahoma at least once a year to attend the Cherokee National Holiday. At home in California, they work with a number of nations native to California, and they have done a great deal of good there. These good people are, in the minds of some, "Wannabes." I can't buy that.

I feel very fortunate that my grandmother was enrolled with the Dawes Commission. I know where her original allotment is, and I know why it is no longer in the family. I know that she attended the Cherokee National Female Seminary and that her father, my great-grandfather, attended and graduated from the Cherokee Male Seminary. I know all this, but even so, if for some reason my grandmother had not got herself enrolled, then I would be in the same shoes as those multitudes of Wannabes.

I feel for them, although most of them do not need my sympathy. They are comfortable in the knowledge that they at least know who they are. I believe them. I believe them unless they give me some reason not to believe them. I especially believe them if they show some real knowledge of Cherokee history and Cherokee culture. I do not have respect for those members of imaginary Cherokee tribes who practice a pseudo-Cherokee culture and sport such made-up Indian-sounding names as Redfeather Thundercloud High Up in a Tree, or whatever. Even if they really do have Cherokee blood in them, they have not done anything to learn anything about their supposed background. They should. They should at least do that much or quit playing Indian games.

So like many other things, I am schizophrenic on this issue. I can see both sides. I can agree to a limited extent with both sides, but I cannot agree completely with either side. Anything to do with American Indians in this country is extremely complex, and I blame the U.S. government for at least 99 percent of that complexity. Some of it is a result of shortsightedness, but more of it is a result of deliberate lies and deceptions. Many of these so-called Wannabes are victims of that history of lies and deception. I said that I believe them. Why shouldn't I? After all, why would anyone these days who is not one want to be a Cherokee?

Oklahoma

I love Oklahoma. I've always loved Oklahoma. When I was ten years old and living with my parents in Okmulgee, my father's employers transferred him to Texas. I can still remember sitting in the backseat of the family car crying as we backed out of the driveway for the last time.

As an adult, when I was working in some other place, like Iowa, and was sent to a conference where I wore a name tag that said underneath my name, "Iowa," and people would look at it and say, "Oh, you're from Iowa," my answer was always, "No. I'm living and working in Iowa right now, but I'm from Oklahoma." I've had a lifelong love affair with Oklahoma.

But having said all of that, I must add that I have no love for the state of Oklahoma. I mean for the state government, the county governments, and the city governments. I have no love for state institutions. I do not root for the Oklahoma Sooners, a football team that proudly wears the designation of not just land stealers but thieves that stole from their own larger band of thieves. (The land-hungry whites who gathered along the Kansas border waiting for the opening of the "Land Rush" to stake their claims on Indian land were called "Boomers." The "Sooners" were those Boomers who sneaked across early to stake their claims.)

I love the land where I was born and where my father was born and his mother before him. I love the people who belong to this land. And for the most part, the people who belong to this land are Native Americans. When I returned to Oklahoma to settle permanently because I no longer felt the need to have a job (by then I was writing full time for a living), I did not feel like I was coming home to Oklahoma so much as I felt like I was coming back to live in the Cherokee Nation.

I live in Tahlequah, the capital city of the Cherokee Nation. It was established as the capital almost immediately following the Cherokee Trail of Tears, the forced removal of the Cherokees from their ancestral homelands in what are now the states of North and South Carolina, Alabama, Georgia, Kentucky, Tennessee, Virginia, and West Virginia. But while that may be the most important part of Oklahoma history for me, it's only a small part of the overall history.

The land we now know as Oklahoma stretches from its neighboring states of Arkansas and Missouri on the east to New Mexico on the west. It's bordered on the north by Kansas and a bit of Colorado and on the south by Texas. In the east it is hilly, sometimes even mountainous, and lush with forests. In the west it is flat, often dry. At the time the United States became interested in this area, it was inhabited and hunted over by Comanches in the south and west, Osages in the northeast, and various Caddoan people, including the Wichita, along the Red River, which is now the border between Oklahoma and Texas.

The land was claimed by the United States in 1803 as part of the larger area known as the Louisiana Purchase. At first, and for a while, it was viewed by the United States as a convenient place to send the unwanted tribes that were located east of the Mississippi River. And although the removal plan was formulated by President Thomas Jefferson as early as 1803, it took the government until the administration of President Andrew Jackson to put the plan into motion. The U.S. Congress passed the Removal Act in 1830, and the Cherokee Nation, the Choctaw Nation, the Creek Nation, the Chickasaw Nation, and the Seminole Nation were all removed into various parts of what is now eastern Oklahoma.

However, a small group of Cherokees had already moved voluntarily into what is now western Arkansas in 1811, and they were recognized by the United States as a separate tribe, called the Cherokee Nation of Indians West of the Mississippi. (They had actually left the old country in 1794 and settled in Missouri until the great 1811 earthquake convinced them to move elsewhere.)

Following the forced removal of the Cherokee Nation in 1838, the United States also coerced the Western Cherokees into moving across the line to be reabsorbed into the larger Cherokee Nation. These five Indian nations, known collectively as "the Five Civilized Tribes," were not placed on reservations. The land they were moved onto was given to them in fee simple title by the United States. The removal treaties promised them that they would never again be disturbed in their sovereignty, and the United States dealt with them as independent republics.

In spite of the hardships of removal, the five nations prospered in their new homes. But the Civil War in the United States brought about many changes. The Confederate States of America talked many Indians from the five tribes into joining the Confederacy. In the case of the Cherokee Nation, these "Confederate" Cherokees had no official position in the government of the Cherokee Nation. They did, however, gather up a strong force, strong enough that the Principal Chief of the Cherokee Nation, John Ross, wrote to Washington asking the U.S. to send troops to protect the nation's neutrality. The United States, though obligated to do so by the removal treaty, refused. Confederate Cherokees under the leadership of General Stand Watie then forced Chief Ross to sign a treaty with the Confederacy. Ross left the Cherokee Nation then, went to Washington, and repudiated the Confederate treaty. The other four nations had similar Civil War experiences.

In spite of the truth of the matter, following the Civil War, the U.S. government used the activities of Confederate Indians as an excuse to force yet another treaty on the five tribes. In this new treaty, Indian Territory was created. The land of the five tribes was consolidated into a territory. That same land is today most of the eastern half of the state of Oklahoma.

The removal frenzy that had begun in 1803 continued. A number of smaller tribes were forced into the extreme northeast corner of "Indian Territory": Peorias, Wyandottes, Ottawas, Shawnees, Senecas, Cayugas, and later even Modocs from northern California. And west of Indian Territory, tribes were moved onto reservations from various parts of the country: Cheyenne and Arapaho, Nez Perce, Pottawatomie, Sac and Fox, Kickapoo, Iowa. In all, it has been said sixty-seven different Indian tribes were moved into what is now Oklahoma from various places. What is now the western part of the state was organized as Oklahoma Territory in 1890. For a time it seemed as if both Indian Territory and Oklahoma Territory were being viewed by the U.S. government as a giant Indian reservation and would stay that way. But such was not the case. As soon as the land that would become Oklahoma was all organized into the two territories, the movement for statehood was under way. The General Allotment Act was passed to allot tribal lands in severalty to individuals (leaving, of course, a large amount of "surplus" land for white settlement), and the Curtis Act was passed later to force the scheme on recalcitrant tribes like the Cherokee Nation.

In 1907, the state of Oklahoma came into being, combining the two territories, Oklahoma Territory and Indian Territory. The theory was that there would be no more Indian tribes in the new state. Everyone was simply a citizen of the state and of the United States. Oklahoma was the great experiment for "getting the government out of the Indian business." In the eastern part of the new state, the former Indian Territory, the business of the transfer of land titles was much more complicated than the government had anticipated, though, and so the governments of the so-called Five Civilized Tribes were continued in a severely limited state. The president of the United States appointed their chiefs. Often in office only long enough to sign some documents, these men became known as "chiefs for a day."

The idea of tribal sovereignty and almost the whole body of federal Indian law were ignored by the new state of Oklahoma. Land grafters set about getting allotted land out of the hands of Indian owners, always unscrupulously, and often brutally. Finally in 1973, President Richard Nixon "gave elections back" to the people of the five tribes, and those nations began a process of revitalizing their tribal governments. Even so, the state did its best to ignore the whole volume of Indian law until recent court cases forced them to begin to recognize tribal rights.

We now have, for the first time since before Oklahoma statehood, a group of young adult Native Americans who have grown up under functioning tribal governments with a state that, however reluctantly, has been recognizing their sovereignty. Nothing is perfect. There are still things to be done, but right now, it seems, they can only get better.

All Indians Are Alike, or "Chiefing"

I don't know when or how it happened. After all, we had James Fenimore Cooper and his Leatherstocking Tales. But somehow the general population of the United States got the impression that all Indians looked and acted like Sioux Indians: Indians on horseback wearing feathered headdresses chasing buffalo across the plains or encircling wagon trains and eventually going home to a circle of tepees. Or at least, as Ralph Friar and Natasha Friar point out in *The Only Good Indian: The Hollywood Gospel*, they all look like Sioux or like Apaches. The Friars maintain that Hollywood had two basic Indian costumes, depending on whether the movie had a big budget or low budget. In low-budget features, an Apache man could be dressed in anything from leggings to a white man's pants, a white man's shirt, and a rag wrapped around the head. Larger-budget westerns could afford to dress the Indians in buckskins with lots of beadwork and elaborate feathered headdresses, like Sioux. Even these two distinctions were often muddled, however, as when an actor would show up dressed like an Apache but wearing a Sioux war bonnet.

The worst case of Hollywood muddling that I ever saw was in an old Roy Rogers movie. (By the way, I've always loved Roy Rogers, and I wish he had not made this movie.) Roy had to go out to the local Indian village, and we see him walking up to the chief, who has just come out of his tepee wearing a Sioux war bonnet (both northern plains items), draped in a Navajo blanket (Southwest), beside a beautiful stream in which is parked a birchbark canoe (Ojibwa from Wisconsin or Minnesota). Oh yeah. There is a totem pole (Northwest) standing beside the tepee. I am not making this up.

These notions go beyond the visual. People often talk about the "Indian language." If they know enough to know that some people speak Cherokee and some speak Cheyenne and some Crow, they may refer to these variations as "dialects of the Indian language." The Indian language and its many dialects are spoken, of course, in India. Not in America. At the time of the arrival of Columbus to these shores, there were something like 1,300 different Indian tribes in what is now North, Central, and South America. Some of these tribes spoke different dialects of the same language. At the same time, there were not only many different languages, but many different language families. For example, Cherokee, Mohawk, Oneida, Onondaga, Seneca, Cayuga, and Tuscarora are all different languages in the Iroquoian language family, just as English, German, Norwegian, Swedish, and Danish are all members of the Germanic language family. Linguists have said that there are Native American languages that are as far from one another as English is from Swahili.

In the not-too-distant past, when Hollywood filmmakers wanted to have a scene in which Indians were speaking their own language, they might have Navajo actors playing Kiowas. It didn't matter. They just told them to speak their language. In one old western movie, the director did such a thing, but when the scene was played back to him, he did not think that the Navajo, or whatever it was, sounded "Indian." He tried several different things, finally telling the Indian actors to just play the scene in English. Then he had the sound track flipped to play it back backward. The backward English sounded "Indian" to him, and that was what wound up in the movie.

Indians cannot grow whiskers, we often hear. The people who believe that statement obviously have not seen the photograph of Satank, the famous Kiowa medicine man. Nor have they seen the numerous pictures taken by Edward Curtis of the Northwest Coast native peoples. They have not yet learned that one of the most popular early trade items from Europe for Indians was a small, tight spring. They liked it because they had been plucking their whiskers with clamshells. They could catch many more whiskers at once with the small spring.

Hollywood filmmakers are probably the greatest villains in this scenario. In films, I have seen Indians dressed like Sioux being called Cherokees. I have written novels about late-nineteenth-century Cherokees in the Cherokee Nation (in what is now northeast Oklahoma) and had New York publishers slap covers on them with pictures of what look like an Apache out on the great desert in Arizona. There used to be, perhaps it still is there, a Cherokee Abstract Company in Tahlequah that had (or still has) as its logo a drawing of an Indian head in a Plains Indian headdress.

One of my major goals as a teacher for nineteen years and, after I quit that dubious profession, as a writer has been to dispel that very popular myth that all Indians are alike. I have tried to write accurately about Cherokees, showing the whole world (I wish the whole world would read my books) that Cherokees are not like Apaches, nor are they like Sioux. So imagine my astonishment the first time I visited Cherokee, North Carolina, and saw a Cherokee Indian on the town's main street, in the height of tourist season, dressed up like a Sioux Indian on the northern plains: full buckskins, beaded moccasins, a full-length headdress, carrying a long staff decorated with animal skins and feathers, and standing in front of a tepee. He was charging tourists money to take his picture.

Here was a Cherokee, on the Cherokee Reservation, in a Cherokee town, doing exactly what the Hollywood filmmakers were doing. Here was a Cherokee feeding the myth that all Indians are alike, enforcing the ignorance that the general public was carrying around in its head, or its many heads. I was sickened. I was disgusted. I was ashamed. I was . . .

Well, before I go on with this, let me tell you about a Creek Indian friend of mine. Some years ago I took a teaching job at Bacone College in Muskogee, Oklahoma. I got to be friends with Gary Colbert, who was the art teacher. Gary is a Creek Indian and a fine artist. Most of his work was then in watercolor. He painted scenes like a Plains Indian burial scaffold. A Plains Indian chasing buffalo. Other Plains Indian scenes. I asked Gary one day, "Why don't you paint any southeastern Indian pictures?" And what do you think he said?

"Because white people want to buy these."

Of course, I couldn't argue. I left Bacone, and about five years later while I was in Sioux City, Iowa, Gary came to town for a visit and brought me a painting of two Creek stickball players. He did not paint it to sell. He gave it to me. I don't know what Gary is selling to white people these days. I've lost track of him. I hope he's selling well.

And, of course, the answer to the practice of "chiefing" in Cherokee, North Carolina, is much the same as Gary's answer about his paintings. John R. Finger, in *Cherokee Americans*, wrote about the practice:

> During the tourist season . . . every morning, like exotic sentries, Cherokee "chiefs" dressed in the war-bonnets of Plains Indians begin their vigils along highways U.S. 441 and U.S. 19. Standing beside little tepees in front of gift shops, they pose for photographs with squealing children and sheepish housewives and assure curious visitors that, yes, they *are* "real" Indians. . . . Henry Lambert has been at it for years, as well as Joseph George and other regulars.[1]

When a Cherokee from North Carolina was asked about another practitioner of that racket, Carl Standingdeer, he gave the following answer. "He's put several kids through college doing that." It's hard to argue with success.

Cherokee Outlaws

My grandfather, Benjamin Franklin Conley, was a master storyteller. Some of the fondest memories of my childhood are of sitting on the porch listening for hours to his tales of early days in Oklahoma (and in Indian Territory before Oklahoma statehood). He remembered the time the Cook brothers stopped at his house for something to eat when he was a child. His mother had seen them coming and had hidden all their money down in the bottom of the flour barrel. She fed them, and they paid her and went on their way.

Later, when Grandpa was a teacher in the Cherokee Nation school at Gideon (in present Cherokee County, Oklahoma), some nephews of Ned Christie were among his pupils, and the Wickliffes used to walk by the schoolhouse occasionally, wearing, he said, long slickers and carrying Winchester rifles. He encountered the U.S. marshal, Gilstrap, while the deputy was en route to his fateful encounter with Charley Wickliffe.

Grandpa's stories held me spellbound, and among other things, they helped turn me into an avid reader of western history at an early age. Naturally, I was particularly fascinated when I ran across stories in print about the same people Grandpa had talked about. I knew that all of these people—Bill and Jim Cook; Charlie, John, and Tom Wickliffe; Ned Christie; Tom, Sam, and Henry Starr; Cherokee Bill—were Cherokees, but that fact failed to impress me much at the time. I suppose, being Cherokee, and having grown up in northeastern Oklahoma, it only seemed natural. I must have been around thirty years old before it occurred to me that the Cherokee tribe of Indians had produced an inordinate number of "outlaws."

About that time, I began to seriously research the subject, and I discovered other Cherokee outlaws: Bob Rogers, Mose Miller,

Zeke Proctor, and Bill Pigeon. At the same time, I found lawmen: Jesse Sunday, Ellis Rattling Gourd, and Sam Sixkiller. And in my own family, there were at least two representatives of that other well-known category of western characters, the crossover category, those who were badmen or lawmen depending on the circumstances, the locale, or their prevailing mood. These were Zeke and Dick Crittenden, members of the posse that accompanied Sheriff Rattling Gourd to the fight at the halfway house where Cherokee Bill killed Deputy Sheriff Sequoyah Houston. Later they posed for the photograph that is usually labeled "The Capture of Cherokee Bill." Eventually, they were gunned down in Wagoner, Indian Territory (now Oklahoma), by Ed Reed, a white man, son of Belle Starr and Jim Reed, in his capacity as deputy marshal.

In other words, I had uncovered a whole crop of Cherokee "gunfighters." To make sure that I had, in fact, come across something of a phenomenon, I delved into the history for the same period of time of the other Indian tribes in what is now Oklahoma. I came across a few comparable characters among the Creeks, Choctaws, and Chickasaws, but nowhere near as many. And among the other tribes, nationwide, there are very few individuals who would be regarded in quite the same way by historians. The Apache Kid is one, perhaps. But the Cherokee case did, in fact, seem to be unique. Why?

After years of research and much thought and soul searching, I think I've come up with the answer, or rather, the answers, for I think that there are four major reasons for the development among the Cherokees of this large group of gunmen. However, before any explanations will make any sense, a bit of Cherokee history needs to be reviewed.

A THUMBNAIL SKETCH OF
CHEROKEE HISTORY

The Cherokees are a large tribe of Native Americans, speaking an Iroquoian language (related to Mohawk, Cayuga, Seneca, Onondaga, Oneida, Tuscarora, and others). Because of this linguistic affiliation to northern tribes and because the Delaware *Walum*

Olum (a tribal narrative chronicle recorded with mnemonic devices and later interpreted, translated, and written down) tells of the Delawares having driven southward a people they call Telega or Tallegewi, supposedly the Cherokees, scholars seem to be in agreement that the Cherokees were originally a northern tribe that migrated to the South. This also, of course, fits with the still widely held notion that all Native Americans migrated generally southward, following their supposed entry into the Americas from Asia by way of the so-called Bering Strait land bridge, a theory never proven, and one that I and other Native Americans (as well as at least one non-Native scholar) dispute. (Jeffrey Goodman, in his book *American Genesis*, argues that the Bering Strait migration went in the opposite direction from what is generally supposed.)

Cherokee oral tradition contains a tale that maintains that the Cherokees came into their historic Smokey Mountain country not from the north, but from an island off the coast of South America, and it is interesting to note, in this vein, that the Cherokee "double weave" basket-making technique is unique among North American Indian tribes but is fairly common in South America.[1]

And, of course, the origin tale gathered by James Mooney on the North Carolina Cherokee reservation during the 1890s and later published in his *Myths of the Cherokees* as "How the World Was Made" would seem to imply that the Cherokees had always been in the region of the Smokey Mountains.[2]

Whatever the case, when we first know of Cherokees historically, they were occupying a vast portion of what is now the southeastern United States, with somewhere between fifty and sixty towns spread throughout all or parts of North Carolina, South Carolina, Tennessee, Kentucky, Virginia, West Virginia, Georgia, and Alabama. Along with their neighboring southeastern tribes, Cherokees apparently built mounds, maintained temples, and lived under a theocracy, being ruled by a powerful priesthood. When the Hernando de Soto expedition went through that territory in 1540, the journals kept reported such sights and spoke of "Kings and Queens."

Cherokee oral tradition (recorded by Mooney) tells of a democratic revolution that occurred when a hunter, returning home after an extended hunting trip, could not find his wife. His neighbors finally told him that during his absence, she had been taken by the priests. Deciding that the powers of the priests had become excessive, the hunter organized his friends and spearheaded a revolution. The priests were all killed.

By the time the English colonies in the South were established, the Cherokees were living in autonomous towns, each governed by two chiefs (a war chief and a peace chief) and a town council. They no longer built mounds or maintained temples. They worshiped, as traditional Cherokees still do, in the open, in outdoor "stomp grounds."

Cherokees encountered Europeans early and had to learn early how to deal with them and how to accommodate them when necessary. And a Cherokee mixed-blood population developed early. Cherokee historian Emmet Starr, in his *History of the Cherokee Indians*, records thirty-seven mixed-blood Cherokee families going back into the 1700s. My own is one of them. When two cultures come into contact with one another, a certain amount of acculturation takes place. Extended trade intensifies this cultural exchange. A significant number of mixed marriages resulting in mixed-blood offspring further increase the assimilation of the group in question. This was the case with the Cherokees in the 1700s, but in the early 1800s something happened to dramatically increase the speed of this process.

When Thomas Jefferson's plan for removing all eastern Indian tribes to locations somewhere west of the Mississippi River became Andrew Jackson's Removal Policy, the Cherokees tried every means of resistance except open warfare. They tried reasoning, pleading, public relations campaigns, lobbying, litigation, and, finally, assimilation. A faction of the Cherokee population, including large numbers of mixed-bloods, believing that the white people of the old South objected to their proximity because of their perceived "savagery," proposed that the Cherokees become "civilized." They launched a planned assimilation campaign. They would imitate the "civilization" of their white neighbors, and then their neighbors would no longer object to their presence. They invited missionaries to the Cherokee country and built churches. They hired teachers from universities in the North and built schools. They raised cattle, hogs, and cotton. (Cherokees had always been farmers.)

The transition from Cherokee matrilineal clans to European-style families with male heads of household, already begun among the mixed-bloods, spread more rapidly. The more aggressive and more successful among the people became wealthy slave-owning plantation dwellers with elaborate antebellum-style homes. They formed the Cherokee Nation with executive, legislative, and judicial branches; voting districts; and a written constitution. The Cherokee Nation began to publish a bilingual newspaper. (Sequoyah had recently presented the people with a syllabary, a writing system for the Cherokee language.)

But they discovered that the idea of Indian removal was not based on concepts of civilization and savagery, for the Cherokees (along with four neighboring tribes that had followed the same path) had become widely known as one of the "Five Civilized Tribes," yet they were still removed. The urgent desire of white Southerners to remove the Indians was based on something other than what the Cherokees had thought. Racism? Perhaps. Land greed? Certainly. And the improvements that the Cherokees had made in their desperate attempt to be seen as desirable neighbors simply made their land more desirable in the eyes of their greedy neighbors.

The story of the Trail of Tears is widely known. In an attempt to legitimize the removal of the Cherokees, the U.S. government negotiated a fraudulent treaty, the Treaty of New Echota, signed on December 29, 1835, with a group of Cherokees not authorized by the government of the Cherokee Nation to do so. These men and their families and friends came to be known as the Treaty Party.

Following the removal, the Cherokees went to work in what is now northeastern Oklahoma to rebuild the Cherokee Nation. What had begun in the Southeast as an attempt to mollify redneck neighbors had become by this time a way of life. Voting districts were drawn up again. A new constitution was written and approved. A national capitol building was erected (which, although it burned and had to be rebuilt once, still stands in Tahlequah, Oklahoma). Wealthier Cherokees built antebellum-style homes. Roads were constructed. Schools and churches were built. The first institution of higher learning west of the Mississippi River was established.

In fact, it might be said that the Cherokees looked at the white man's civilization and then set about improving on it. They saw it not only for what it was, but also for what it was supposed to be, and they imitated the ideal. The highest item on the national budget was education. The Cherokee National Council (the legislative body) was forbidden by the constitution to vote itself a raise. There was no national debt.

By 1907, when the state of Oklahoma came into being and took over the Cherokee school system (probably the first free, compulsory public education system in this country, perhaps the world), the Cherokee Nation had produced more college graduates than its neighboring states of Arkansas and Texas combined. Cherokees imitated the white man well, but the white man had something else the Cherokees had not had before contact, before this long and strange process of cultural assimilation, something besides fine homes, bank accounts, churches, schools, and voting districts. The white people had their outlaws, and the new Cherokee society, a true microcosm, would have them too.

IMITATING THE WHITE MAN

Senator Henry Dawes of Massachusetts, visiting the Cherokee Nation in preparation for the writing of what would become the General Allotment Act, or the Dawes Act, said of the Cherokee Nation that

> there was not a family in that whole Nation that had not a home of its own. There was not a pauper in that Nation, and the Nation did not owe a dollar. It built its own capitol . . . and it built its schools and its hospitals. Yet the defect of the system was apparent. They have got as far as they can go, because they own their land in common . . . there is no enterprise to make your home any better than that of your neighbors. There is no selfishness, which is at the bottom of civilization.[3]

This was, of course, his justification for making private land-owners out of Indians. Be that as it may, there was another side of this imitation white society that Henry Dawes failed to notice, or at least failed to note. The white frontier had its churches and schools, its prosperous businessmen, but it also had its ne'er-do-wells, its misfits, its bums, drunks, and outlaws. The Cherokee Nation, in modeling itself after the United States, produced its own social deviants as well.

The old tribal system no longer worked to maintain harmony and balance. Too much of it was gone. The clan system, under-mined by adaptation to the European-style bilateral family, lost its controlling and ordering functions. Something had to replace it, and the thing that was chosen to replace it was the same thing that white people used, an institutionalized legal system with its laws made by a legislative body, law enforcement officers to arrest those who violated those laws, and courts to determine guilt or innocence and to decree punishment of the guilty.

And the system produced some outstanding men: legislators like Clement Vann Rogers (the father of Will Rogers and the man for whom Rogers County, Oklahoma, is named), Ned Christie, (before an incident, or plot—but more on that later—changed the direction of his career), George Washington (Wash) Swimmer, and Rabbit Bunch; judges like Osceola Benge, Bluford West, and Henry Clay Ross; lawmen like Sequoyah Houston (killed by Cherokee Bill at the famous gunfight at Effie Crittenden's halfway house on Fourteen Mile Creek) and Samuel Sixkiller and Jesse Sunday (both murdered, shot from ambush after distinguished careers as district sheriffs); and outlaws.

Cherokee Bill, whose real name was Crawford Goldsby, was a Cherokee citizen said to have been a mixture of Cherokee, Sioux, black, white, and Mexican, "with all the worse qualities of each race." He was a bad outlaw at an early age. He's also an unusual outlaw in that, so far as I know, no writer has ever attempted to defend him or to turn him into a good boy gone bad because of the forces of society. He was hanged for murder at Fort Smith, and no one seems ever to have argued that he shouldn't have been, with the exceptions of his mother, his younger brother, and his lawyer.

There were the Cook brothers, Bill and Jim, also mixed-bloods. They were associated briefly with Cherokee Bill. Young Jim's outlaw career was very short. He was badly wounded in the same fight that cost the life of Deputy Sheriff Sequoyah Houston, and his brother had to leave him behind. The elder Cook's career as a fugitive seems to have outlasted his outlaw career. Eventually arrested in New Mexico, where he was working as a cowboy (another favorite Cherokee occupation in those days), he spent the rest of his life in a federal prison.

Bob Rogers seems to have been an overgrown, spoiled child, who finally went too far. He was killed in a gun battle with lawmen.

These men seem to have been genuine outlaws. By that I mean that they seem to have been men who just had a mean streak or wanted easy money or cheap thrills. None of them were full-blood Cherokees. They were products of the frontier who happened to have some Cherokee blood and had been born in the Cherokee Nation, so were citizens. They were typical frontier products, more like the James and Younger brothers, the Daltons, or the Renos than anyone else. And those outlaws, or others like them (for there were large numbers of white people in the Cherokee Nation in those days), were probably their models.

TWO CIVIL WARS

Civil wars have a way of producing outlaws, and the Cherokee Nation suffered two civil wars, one almost on the heels of the other. It has been said, and it's probably true, that there is not one Cherokee family that escaped tragedy in connection with the Trail of Tears. My wife and I have in our possession, from her family papers, some pages from a family Bible that record the death of a six-year-old child in prison on the banks of the Hiwassee River in Georgia while awaiting removal, and thousands died on the trail.

The members of the Treaty Party had immigrated early, almost immediately after the signing of the treaty, and they had moved under better circumstances and with much more comfort than the majority who followed in their footsteps under a forced removal. In the early 1840s, following the arrival of the main body of Cherokees over the Trail of Tears, those who had suffered that forced removal began a systematic killing of the signers of the treaty.

Elias Boudinot was hacked to death in front of his house. Major Ridge was shot off his horse from ambush. John Ridge, his son, was dragged from his sick bed and stabbed many times in front of his helpless wife and child. The son, John Rollin Ridge, grew up harboring thoughts of revenge, but he never managed to even attempt to carry out any of his plots. He eventually moved to California, where he became celebrated as the author of *The Life and Adventures of Joaquin Murieta the Celebrated California Bandit* under the pen name (his Cherokee name) of Yellow Bird.

Another treaty signer killed in front of members of his family at his own home was James Starr. A surviving witness was his son, Tom. Tom Starr vowed massive revenge, and legend says that before he stopped, Tom Starr had killed one hundred men. The Cherokee Nation put a price on Tom's head, and Tom built an outlaw stronghold. It was to this place that the young white woman from Missouri, Myra Belle Shirley, came when she married Tom's son, Sam.

The civil war between the members of the Treaty Party and the other faction, known variously as the Ross Party or the National Party, eventually died down, but when the U.S. Civil War broke out, the flames of the old Cherokee civil war were rekindled. The Treaty Party people were largely mixed-bloods who had been plantation owners in the old South. The Ross Party was made up mostly of more traditional full-blood Cherokees.

With the Civil War, the Treaty Party became "Confederate Cherokees." At first the Cherokee Nation under the leadership of Principal Chief John Ross attempted to remain neutral. Chief Ross, in fact, pleaded with the United States to send troops to the Cherokee Nation to ensure and protect its neutrality. When the government failed to respond to the plea, Cherokee Union troops were organized, and the Cherokee Nation had a microcosm within it of the larger Civil War that was raging outside its boundaries. The labels had changed, but it was the old Cherokee civil war all over again.

The Starr family of outlaws was a product of all this violence. Tom Starr, who lived to a ripe old age and died in bed, eventually made his peace with the Cherokee Nation, but he had lived the life of an outlaw for too long. His son, Sam, followed in his footsteps. Lacking his father's sense of mission and strength of character, Sam comes across as a cheap horse thief, and his marriage to Myra Belle and association with her activities and her legend (Belle Starr, the Outlaw Queen) certainly do not help his image.

Henry Starr was the son of another of Tom's sons, George "Hop" Starr. Henry's outlaw career, however, is entirely his own. He lived farther north than did his grandfather and his uncles, and he left home at an early age to escape the tyranny of a white stepfather. He found work as a cowboy on various ranches in the northwestern reaches of the Cherokee Nation. According to Henry's own story, *Thrilling Events*, written while he was in prison in Colorado and published in Tulsa, Oklahoma, in 1913, he was twice arrested on false charges, perhaps just because of his name. Humiliated because of his jail experience, he decided that if he was going to have the reputation of being an outlaw, he might as well really be one. He began by robbing railroad depots and country stores, but he soon graduated to banks. He seems to have developed a fascination for bank robbery.

Henry Starr is said to have robbed more banks than any man in history (a claim he himself made on his deathbed), and he successfully planned the simultaneous robbery of two banks, a feat that had proved disastrous to the famous Dalton gang. Henry was wounded and captured on this occasion, but the banks were robbed, and members of his gang escaped with the loot. Henry Starr, perhaps the most colorful and intriguing of all this group of outlaws, began his career in the 1890s on horseback and continued off and on until he was killed attempting to rob a bank in Arkansas in 1921, having driven to town in a Ford car. He was the first and only person ever killed during a Henry Starr robbery.

JURISDICTIONAL CONFUSION

Perhaps the Cherokees would have been able to successfully establish their amalgam of Cherokee and white civilization and develop the near utopia seen by Henry Dawes without having to put up with the accompanying lawlessness had it not been for more interference from the government of the United States. The federal court at Fort Smith, Arkansas, presided over by Judge Isaac C. Parker, has been a subject of controversy since its inception. Judge Parker has been seen as a monster who longed for a record of having hanged a hundred men, and he has been seen as the harbinger of law and order to a territory rife with lawlessness and violence, the savior of the Indians. One point of view that has not been much explored, however, is that of the Indian Nations in the so-called Indian Territory. Present remarks will be limited to the Cherokee Nation.

The Cherokee Nation, as has been earlier noted, had a complete legal system. It had its constitution, its laws, its law enforcement officers, and its court system, including a supreme court. All were functioning. All were efficient.

The U.S. court at Fort Smith was established because of the uncontrolled violence in Indian Territory. How can these two statements both be true? The answer is simple. The U.S. government decreed that the Cherokee courts had no jurisdiction over crimes involving white people. And there were large numbers of white people in the Cherokee Nation. In addition, with such a decree, the territory of the Cherokee Nation became more attractive to outlaws of every stripe.

So the U.S. government with its jurisdictional decree created a situation of uncontrolled violence in the Cherokee Nation, then used that situation as an excuse to further establish its own jurisdiction over the territory. The two best-known stories involving Cherokee "outlaws" to come about directly as a result of this jurisdictional confusion are those of Wili Woyi (or Bill Pigeon) and Zeke Proctor.

Bill Pigeon had killed a man who was attempting to rob him at his home. He believed the man to be a citizen of the Cherokee

Nation. (The citizenship rolls of the Cherokee Nation included full-blood Cherokees, mixed-blood Cherokees, white people married to Cherokees, white people adopted or naturalized as citizens, and former black slaves, called on the rolls "Freedmen.") Bill Pigeon turned himself in to Cherokee authorities. His trial date was set in the Cherokee Nation courts, and he was on his way to the trial when he received word that it had been determined that the man he had killed was not, after all, a Cherokee citizen, and that the trial would not take place. Instead, a deputy U.S. marshal was waiting for him at the courthouse with a federal warrant.

Bill Pigeon had no faith in the white people's courts, so he turned around and went back home. (It may be that he also thought that the courts of the U.S. government had no right interfering with the business of the Cherokee Nation, the internal affairs of the Cherokee Nation. More on this later.)

Judge Parker's deputies searched in vain for Bill Pigeon for eleven years. They finally found a badly decomposed body and declared it to be his in order to close the case. According to Cherokee tradition, Bill Pigeon was never caught because he was a powerful Indian doctor, or medicine man, who could, among other things, make himself invisible.

Zeke Proctor became a wanted man following his accidental fatal shooting of a Cherokee woman, Polly Beck Hildebrand. Zeke's brother-in-law, a white man named James Kesterson, had abandoned Zeke's sister with her small child. Then he had moved in with another Cherokee woman, Polly Beck Hildebrand. Zeke confronted Kesterson in a rage, and Kesterson went for his gun. Zeke beat Kesterson to the draw, but the woman jumped in front of Kesterson and was killed by Zeke's bullet. Kesterson ran away unharmed. Zeke turned himself in to Cherokee authorities. Relatives of the dead woman, fearing that Zeke would not be convicted, went to Fort Smith with Kesterson and charged Zeke with the attempted murder of a white man.

A federal warrant was issued for Zeke's arrest, but the deputy carrying the warrant was instructed to allow the Cherokee trial to go on. If the Cherokee court convicted Zeke of murder and sentenced him to hang, everything would be all right. But if Zeke was acquitted, the deputy was to arrest him on the federal charge.

The controversial trial of Zeke Proctor in the Cherokee Nation court led to a bloody gunfight in the courthouse during the trial. During the fight, Zeke escaped and became a fugitive. The Cherokee court was reconvened hastily and almost in secret the next day, and Zeke was found innocent of murder. However, the federal court in Fort Smith had issued murder warrants against Zeke, the judge, and the jury for the deaths that occurred during the battle. The Cherokee Nation took the position that Zeke Proctor had been tried and found not guilty of the killing of Polly Beck Hildebrand, that the incident had fallen rightfully under the jurisdiction of the Cherokee Nation, and that Kesterson had become a citizen of the Cherokee Nation as a result of his marriage to Zeke's sister. The U.S. courts had no jurisdiction.

The U.S. government thought differently, however, and federal deputies continued to search for Zeke. In the meantime, the Cherokee Nation issued warrants for the arrest of members of the Beck family, the relatives of the dead woman, for the killings at the courthouse. The Becks fled across the border into Arkansas. Some federal officials at Fort Smith requested that U.S. troops be sent in, but, happily, cooler heads prevailed. At last, the warrants were recalled on both sides, and the whole affair was dropped.

Zeke Proctor led a long and productive life after that episode. He was a prosperous farmer, and he was even a peace officer. He had been a fugitive, and he had been called an outlaw. But his "outlaw" career was a direct result of the jurisdictional confusion brought about by the U.S. government.

POLITICS AND THE NIGHTHAWKS

There are various stories regarding the origin of the Keetoowah Society and the Nighthawk Keetoowahs among the Cherokees. Some say that the Keetoowahs are an ancient society, others that they were organized as late as 1859. There is a story that the Nighthawks developed as a result of a split in the original Keetoowah

Society. Suffice it to say here that the Nighthawk Keetoowahs, in the latter half of the nineteenth century in the Cherokee Nation, were a secret, full-blood Cherokee society dedicated to preserving Cherokee culture, traditions, and national integrity.

The Nighthawks were opposed to the idea of the allotment of Cherokee lands to individuals. They were opposed to any encroachment of the U.S. government into the jurisdiction of the Cherokee Nation. They were opposed to the movement for Oklahoma statehood. The Nighthawks were a nationalistic society of Cherokee patriots.

The story of Zeke Proctor takes on additional meaning when it is known that he was associated with the Nighthawks. Being a Nighthawk, Zeke had political reasons to ignore the authority of the federal court. His political philosophy denied that the U.S. government had any authority over Cherokees.

The idea of Oklahoma statehood was totally bound up with the idea of the destruction of the Indian nations in what would become Oklahoma. The tribal governments needed to be dissolved. Property needed to change hands. Since there was no place left to move the Cherokees to, they had to be provided for within the limits of the new state. They would be made private landowners and individual citizens of the state. There were to be no more Indian tribes in Oklahoma and no more Indians. The Nighthawks were a strong force of resistance to all of these ideas. I will return to the Nighthawks shortly.

One of the most written about of the Cherokee "outlaws" is Ned Christie. Several standard histories of the period call him something like the worst outlaw ever to roam Indian Territory. He is accused by many different writers of having committed numerous murders, robberies, rapes, and other crimes. The standard version of the Ned Christie story runs something like this.

Ned Christie, a full-blood Cherokee fluent in both Cherokee and English, was a blacksmith and gunsmith. Elected to the Cherokee National Council, he might have been a useful citizen had it not been for one thing. Like all Indians, they say, he could not hold his liquor. One night when he was drunk in Tahlequah, he shot and killed Deputy U.S. Marshal Dan Maples. When he sobered up, he ran away to the hills. Sometime during the next few years, in an encounter with another deputy marshal, he and the deputy shot and wounded each other. The deputy was shot through the hips and retired from service. Christie was shot in the face. He swore never to speak English again. Five years after the killing of Maples, a posse of twenty-three deputies surrounded Christie in his home, and after an all-night battle, which included the use of a field cannon and dynamite against Christie, they killed him.

I was always curious as to why, if Ned Christie committed such an incredible number of horrible crimes, none of these writers ever bothered to tell me what any of those crimes had been. Some years ago, I attempted to research the life of Ned Christie, and I was unable to find one crime attributed to him, other than the killing of Dan Maples and resisting arrest. I did find in my research some serious doubt as to whether Christie even actually shot Maples. Anyone who has read the works of those writers called by Emmet Starr "Two-Gun Historians" has come across descriptions of the robberies committed by Jesse James, the Daltons, Henry Starr, and others. The accounts tell not only what banks they robbed, but also what dates they robbed them, what time they rode into town, the name of the teller who was on duty in the bank, on which side of the street they tied their horses, and how much money, to the penny, they rode away with.

Needless to say, I found a serious deficiency in the Ned Christie stories. I began to doubt that he was, after all, the worst outlaw ever to roam Indian Territory. What was going on?

According to the Two-Gun Historians, Mose Miller was another bad, full-blood Cherokee outlaw. I have read two absolutely different accounts of his outlaw career. Like the standard Ned Christie story, these stories do not attribute specific crimes to Mose Miller. Even so, the two stories constantly contradict each other. Mose Miller is not as widely talked about among Cherokees today as is Ned Christie, nor is he much written about. It is more difficult to find anything substantial to say about him. But for my purposes here, he is another full-blood Cherokee who has been called a bad outlaw and about whom the stories just don't quite add up.

Charley Wickliffe is yet another. Charley was wanted for killing deputy marshals—nothing else. I've always wanted to know why he killed that first one. Charley is said to have been a bad outlaw. He liked to kill deputy marshals. He traveled around with his two brothers, John and Tom, and now and then he would kill a deputy. Eventually, John and Tom wandered into town and said that Charley was dead. They had only gone around with him, they said. They had never killed anyone. The case was closed. The Wickliffes were full-bloods, and their story, as it is generally presented, is more than a bit puzzling.

But a puzzle can be solved, and these three stories have several things in common. They are all about traditional, full-blood Cherokees. (With the exceptions of Zeke Proctor and Bill Pigeon, none of the other outlaws dealt with herein were full-bloods, and I intend to show that these two men have more in common with these last three men than may be immediately apparent.) Ned Christie, Mose Miller, and Charley Wickliffe are all generally presented as exceptionally bad outlaws, yet all three stories about them are vague in terms of just what these three men had done to merit such a label. And the stories all take place in the late 1880s and in the 1890s (Charley Wickliffe's case was not actually resolved until 1906, the year before Oklahoma statehood), the time during which the enrollment officers were busy assigning allotments to Cherokees in preparation for the final destruction of the Cherokee Nation and the emergence of the state of Oklahoma.

I am happy to be able to report here that since my initial unsuccessful efforts at researching the Ned Christie story some years ago, two more diligent researchers than I have done the job. Among other things, they reported that Ned Christie and Charley Wickliffe, as well as Zeke Proctor, were Nighthawks, and a photograph of Mose Miller wearing a Nighthawk sash has been published. Both writers also determined the identity of the real killer of Dan Maples, and it was not Ned Christie.

These so-called full-blood Cherokee outlaws were all Nighthawks, active in resisting the movement for allotment and for Oklahoma statehood. (Bill Pigeon may or may not have been a Nighthawk, but being a traditional Cherokee Indian doctor, it is likely that he was. His sympathies and his philosophy certainly agreed with theirs.[4])

Is it not possible, or even probable, that the same government that had created within the borders of the Cherokee Nation a lawless territory by denying that nation the right to police its own lands, then used that very lawlessness as an excuse for imposing its own jurisdiction in that territory and was carrying that process even further by passing laws to dissolve the Cherokee Nation and deny the tribal existence of the Cherokee people—is it not possible and even probable that same government would find a way to destroy its opposition's most vocal and influential leaders? I believe that to be the case. I believe that Ned Christie, Mose Miller, Charlie Wickliffe, Zeke Proctor, and Bill Pigeon, the so-called full-blood Cherokee outlaws, were not outlaws at all. I believe they were Cherokee patriots dedicated to the preservation of the Cherokee Nation. I further believe they were victims—singled out, labeled as outlaws, and pursued as outlaws in order to silence their political interference with the process of fulfilling what the U.S. government viewed as its manifest destiny.

So there is not one answer to the question originally posed by this essay: Why did the Cherokee Nation produce so many outlaws? There are at least four answers. The Cherokee Nation in many ways mirrored the frontier communities of the United States, and so contained some of the same kind of social misfits. The years of civil unrest, including Cherokee participation in the U.S. Civil War, produced outlaws, just as the Civil War produced outlaws, such as the James and Younger gangs, outside the Cherokee Nation. The jurisdictional confusion created by the U.S. government, seemingly on purpose and with devious intent, created outlaws in the eyes of the U.S. government but not in the eyes of the Cherokee Nation. And finally, Cherokee patriots who were viewed as problems by the U.S. government were conveniently labeled outlaws and hunted down to remove their opposition.

Grafters, Sooners, and Other Crooks

I do not go to University of Oklahoma football games. I do not support the Sooners. I occasionally watch a Sooner game on television hoping to see the Sooners defeated. If they get too far ahead of the other team, and the situation appears to be hopeless, I change the channel. It's not that I have no pride in the University of Oklahoma. It's a great institution, and it operates a great press. I have published several books with the University of Oklahoma Press. I am pleased at the recent move of the press to a location off campus, because it always pissed me off a bit when I visited the press, in its old location, to see the small press building in the shadow of the huge football stadium. I would support the University of Oklahoma football team anyway, though, if it had another name. Gophers, maybe. I don't care. Almost anything but Sooners.

Why do I dislike that name so much? The answer is simple. Sooners is a name for which most people have forgotten the meaning, or they never knew it. It's a name of significant historical meaning. It's a name much like its cousin, "grafters." We have sort of forgotten "grafters." We would probably have forgotten it altogether had not Angie Debo written *And Still the Waters Run*. In that landmark book, Debo writes:

> During the decade that elapsed from the abolition of tribal status by the Curtis Act to the creation of a state government, the bulk of the landed wealth of the Indians passed into individual hands. The Indians had been independent and self-sustaining under an economic order which they understood, but to a great majority the new status carried conceptions of property entirely foreign to their previous experience. As the

business incapacity of the allottees became apparent, a horde
of despoilers fastened themselves upon their property.

. . . The plunder of Indians was so closely joined with
pride in the creation of a great new commonwealth that it
received little condemnation. The term "grafter" was applied
as a matter of course to dealers in Indian land, and was
frankly accepted by them.[1]

They were proud of being grafters. I won't go further into their
methods or the tremendous amount of thievery they accomplished.
If you are not familiar with this period of Oklahoma history, read
Debo's book. It should be required reading for all Oklahomans.
Know what it is you're being proud of.

So what has all of that to do with my attitude toward Sooners?
Just this. Pride in the term "Sooners" is exactly comparable to pride
in the term "grafters." "Sooners" is a derogatory term, downright
insulting. It's not quite as low as child molester, woman killer, or
son of a bitch, but it's damn low on the list. Where did it come
from, and what does it mean?

Following the Civil War, the U.S. government forced several
Indian tribes to give up land amounting to two million acres in the
center of what is now the state of Oklahoma, presumably because
of their involvement with the Confederacy. This land became
known as the Unassigned Lands. A Kansan named David L. Payne,
in the 1870s, organized a group that became known as the Boomers
to settle the Unassigned Lands. In 1879, Payne led the Boomers to
an area in what is now Oklahoma City and settled a town called
Ewing. Soon the U.S. Army arrested them and removed them back
to Kansas. They returned to Ewing and were arrested again. This
time they were taken to Fort Smith, Arkansas, to be tried in federal
court. They were found guilty and fined, but the fine was never
collected, and nothing came of it.

Payne tried one more invasion with his Boomers, this time in
1884 into the Cherokee Outlet. He was arrested again, and the
Boomers were evicted. He was taken again to Fort Smith, but for
some reason the trial was moved to federal court in Kansas, where
the court ruled that settling on the Unassigned Lands was not a

criminal offense. Payne was freed. Payne died before the first legal invasion, but his Boomers lived on. Their late leader has since been called the Father of Oklahoma, the Oklahoma Moses, Prince Boomer, the Cimarron Scout, Oklahoma Payne, and Ox Heart. The followers of Ox Heart, the Boomers, finally won out. In 1889, the Unassigned Lands were opened for white settlement.

Thousands of lusty and lustful Boomers lined up on the border in Kansas, just north of the Unassigned Lands, waiting for the gunshot that would turn them loose for the great land run, racing for the best piece of land in wagons, on horseback, on bicycles, on foot. The Boomers waited for the free Indian land. Most of them.

Some Boomers—not content with the disagreeable name of Boomer, not content to wait, certainly not content to play fair—sneaked across the line early to stake their claims. They were called Sooners, and at the time, Sooner was as low a name as one could be given. A Sooner was a thief who stole from his own buddies, who were stealing from Indians.

In William S. Hart's once famous but now nearly forgotten silent film *Tumbleweeds* (1925), the 1889 land run is a major plot ingredient. At one point the Hart character is falsely accused of being a Sooner and is thrown with many other Sooners into a stockade jail, where he is ridiculed, spat at, and threatened with lynching. Yet in 1908, only nineteen years after the land run, and one year into Oklahoma statehood, the University of Oklahoma named its teams Sooners. Like grafters, Sooners had become a name to be proud of. There is currently a University of Oklahoma Sooners Web site that defines Sooner as "a synonym for Progressivism. The Sooner is an 'energetic individual who travels ahead of the human procession.'" A nice redefinition of a cheat and a sneak thief, don't you think? I think there is no state in the United States that shows more pride in its crooked, self-serving, cheating, and corrupt founding fathers than Oklahoma.

At this point, I think it is necessary for me to point out that I am not writing from an "Indian point of view," neither am I writing from a "Cherokee point of view." I am writing from my own personal point of view. I know Indians, lots of them, who proudly display Sooners propaganda: bumper stickers, hats, sweatshirts, shoes. Sooners. Sooners. Sooners. Their favorite topic of conversation is what the Sooners are doing, how they are doing, what they should be doing.

I expressed my opinion of the Sooners to a Choctaw friend of mine one time. This Choctaw is a big-time Sooner fan, and he waited patiently until I had run out of breath. Then he said, regarding the land run of 1889, "There wasn't no Choctaw land involved in that."

I have been told that most people today, including most University of Oklahoma football players, probably have no idea what Sooner means. That may be. Then I still refuse to support them. Ignorance is no excuse. They should find out what it means. Until they do, and until the name changes, I will remain an enthusiastic fan of whatever team happens to be playing against the Sooners.

Why the DAR Did Not Like Me

I spent nine years in Sioux City, Iowa, as director of the Indian Studies Program at Morningside College. While I was there, I was invited to speak to the local chapter of the Daughters of the American Revolution (DAR), for what reason I do not know or do not remember. I also do not recall what the topic of my speech was, but I do recall that early in the speech, probably in some introductory comments intended to loosen things up, I made the following casual remark. "I had ancestors in the American Revolution, but they were on the other side." The audience immediately turned against me. I could see it in their faces, which, by the way, had not been overly friendly even before my smart-assed comment.

Their minds did not change, either, after I had explained that my ancestor, Richard Pearis, was an Irishman who was licensed by the colony of North Carolina to trade with the Cherokees. When the American Revolution broke out, Pearis stayed loyal to the British Crown. A substantial faction of Cherokees, under the leadership of Tsiyu-Gansini, or Dragging Canoe, also chose to fight alongside the British against the Americans. I don't know Richard Pearis's motivations, but the motivations of the Cherokees are clear. The king of England was trying to contain the colonies along the eastern seaboard, while the Americans wanted to move out onto Indian land. Some already had. The interests of the Cherokees (and of other Indians) were obviously in line with those of the British.

This explanation did not temper the reaction of the members of the DAR, however. They paid little attention to anything else I had to say. All their faces were drawn. Their brows were knit. Their lips were pursed. No one had a single kind or friendly remark to say to me as I left the room following my talk. There are certain things that white people do not like to hear Indians say.

Some years and a previous wife earlier, I was in Billings, Montana, at then Eastern Montana College, with the improbable title of Coordinator of Indian Culture. I was driving somewhere with a good friend of mine, an Assiniboine Indian from Fort Belknap in Montana. We passed a billboard sign with some purposely misspelled words on it. I don't remember the words, but they were in the same category as "Hep-U-Sef" gasoline, which I had seen on a billboard some years earlier in Missouri. My friend said to me, "Look at that. These white people are fucking up the English language."

I roared with laughter. I thought it was hilarious. When I got home later in the day, I told my then wife, a white woman from Texas, the story, thinking that she, too, would find it amusing. She did not. She looked at me with a scowl on her face and said, "Well. It's our language."

Back to Sioux City. I was team-teaching a summer class in human relations with a white woman from the education department to a group of schoolteachers. I'm not at all sure of the sequence of the following events, but I do remember both of them clearly. I was discussing symbolism and how it means different things to people of different backgrounds, different cultures. There was a television commercial being shown in those days for some life insurance company. To emphasize the feeling of security one should get from being insured by this outfit, the commercial showed a troop of blue-coated cavalry riding straight at the camera, while in the background a bugle was playing "Gary Owen." (This was Custer's favorite tune, the one he always had played for a charge.)

I said that where those symbols might work for white people, they surely would not work for Indians. For Indians, they would conjure up an entirely different image, an image of terror. When I was through with my talk, a woman came up to speak to me. She said that she was never a racist until that day. I had made her a racist by talking about the U.S. Cavalry attacking those helpless

Indian villages and all. Things I had never mentioned. She must have known about them though. They were in her mind.

On another occasion, in that same class, I was talking about the concept of dual citizenship. I told them, for example, that I was a Cherokee citizen and I was also a citizen of the United States. After my explanation, someone in the class asked me if I had to choose between the two, which would I choose. I told them that I was a Cherokee first, and that would be my choice. Now here's the upshot of those two incidents.

We assigned a paper in that class. The class had about forty students (teachers). We divided the papers in half. I took half of them to grade, and the other teacher took the other half. When we had them all marked and graded, we returned them to the students. Students whose papers I had graded, when they had questions about the things I had marked, took the papers to the other teacher for explanations! They resented the fact that I had marked their English usage! Like the time my wife said, "It's our language."

Trying to make some sense out of all this, I decided that even when white people don't know their history all that well, they do know enough to be aware of the fact that the United States often did the Indians dirty. White people were not always angelic. Therefore, when anyone, particularly an Indian, reminds them of that fact of history, they resent it. They become defensive. If they're smart enough, they do a little juggling of the facts, like a few years ago, when some western writers I know accused some writers, including some Indian writers, of writing "revisionist history." It's true, they said, that bad things were done by whites against Indians, but Indians also did some bad things to whites, ignoring the fact that throughout the so-called Indian wars, Indians were defending their own land. White people were invaders.

And what about the language? That one is a little trickier. Many white people, including that one-time wife of mine, are as far removed from their original languages as I am from the Cherokee language. English is the only language I speak. But Cherokee is my language. I think it was stolen from me. My ex-wife's family's language was Czech. She couldn't speak that either. The people in the classroom I had so much trouble with were descendants of Swedes, Norwegians, Fins, and Germans—few, if any, were of English descent. But they are white Americans, and English is their language. Woe to any American Indian who dares to claim it as his or her own.

Finally, how dare I, according to the DAR, question the divine motives of the Founding Fathers? "Give me liberty or give me death," cried Patrick Henry, who was deeply in debt in England. It's the Boston Tea Party against "Mad" King George. It was a totally justifiable and justified revolution. Probably the only one in the history of the world. Don't remind the DAR of the black slaves. Don't remind them that there were Indians living here first who wanted to save their own lands and their own lifeways—their own liberties. Don't remind them of broken treaties.

It was not ignorance that caused so many writers of high school textbooks of American history to compose books that did not mention American Indians. Instead of discussing the taking of Indian lands to create the United States, they discussed the hardy pioneers conquering the wilderness (uninhabited land). They did talk about getting lands away from France (the Louisiana Purchase) and away from Mexico and Russia. Indians did not come into play in these stories. Many white Americans would like to hold on to this history. They would prefer to believe that their ancestors rode into a vast wilderness, that there were no Indian people on this continent, or, at the very least, that the Indians really were the ignorant and cruel savages depicted in much popular literature and in the movies.

The twisting of history and the use (or misuse) of language are entangled. If one has an image of American Indians as ignorant savages or as nonexistent, then it must be indeed appalling to have an Indian correct one's English. Or conversely, if Indians are intelligent enough to master the English language, often better than white people, then how can the Indians of the history books be the savages that white people want them to be?

Margot Astrov wrote, in a marvelous book originally called *The Winged Serpent,* and later retitled *American Indian Prose and Poetry,*

that to American Indians, "language was sacred." If only that attitude could be revived, and if only it could spread to other races,
that would go a long ways toward solving the problems of white
people's attitudes toward both history and language.

Cherokee Women and the Clan System

Speaking to the Cherokee Council and the U.S. Treaty Commission in 1781, Nancy Ward, the Beloved Woman, said, "You know that women are always looked upon as nothing; but we are your mothers; you are our sons."

This was an incredibly profound statement, a blunt comment on the truth of a change that had already taken place in Cherokee society, a change that would affect Cherokee life, all of Cherokee life, from then on. Nancy Ward, Nanye-hi, represented the last vestiges of an old lifestyle.

From as far back as we know anything of the Cherokees, Cherokee society was organized by clans. A clan is a family that determines descent through one line or the other but not through both. There are matrilineal and patrilineal clans. Cherokee clans are matrilineal. That means that children are all born into their mother's clan. It also means that fathers are almost irrelevant. The father belongs to his mother's clan. He is not even a member of the family. He can be easily discarded.

There are seven Cherokee clans: *ani-tsisqua* (bird), *ani-waya* (wolf), *ani-kawi* (deer), *ani-wodi* (paint), *ani-sakoni* (blue), *ani-gatagewi* (wild potato), and *ani-gilohi* (long hair). Every Cherokee belonged to one of these clans. According to the old clan system, a child born to a Cherokee mother and a white father, even though the child is but 1/32 Cherokee by blood, is a Cherokee, whereas a child born to a Cherokee father and a white woman, though the child be half Cherokee by blood, is not a Cherokee. So the issue in the old days was not race, and not blood degree, but clan affiliation. And even though the Cherokees were scattered throughout an area that has become eight or so states in some two hundred towns, the same seven clans were represented in every Cherokee town. A Cherokee could travel hundreds of miles to a Cherokee town where he or she had never been before and find relatives, clan members.

Many things that to white people, and now to all of us, are matters for the state (the legal system) to decide were, in the old days when Cherokee clans were fully functioning, matters for the clans (clan law). For example, to use an extreme, if a Cherokee from the Bird Clan killed a Cherokee from the Wolf Clan, it was up to the Wolf Clan members to exact balance, that is, to claim a life from the Bird Clan.

Cherokee women were the clan leaders. A married man moved in with his wife and his wife's clan. The woman owned the house. She owned the garden. An old woman of the clan, probably the head of the clan, at least in her town, gave a clan name to a newborn child. And women had political power. When the chiefs were male, and only men served on the councils, where did this political power reside? We don't know exactly. The structure of the old Cherokee town government (and the towns were autonomous—there was no central government) is not well known to us today. There is speculation. But there were probably female advisers to the chiefs (a war chief and a peace chief) and to the council. We do know the following.

Early European comments on Cherokee behavior reveal much. One wag said, "The Cherokees have a petticoat government." This was probably an astute observation. Another wry comment was, "Among the Cherokees the women [*sic*] rules the roost." Most likely equally accurate. What had happened, apparently, was that the white men would meet with the Cherokee men to decide something between them, and the Cherokee men would suggest that they meet again in, say, four days. At the second meeting, the Cherokee men would give their decision. It took the white men a while to figure out that the Cherokee men were not simply unable to make up their minds. Rather, they had to go home to discuss the matter with their women before coming to a decision. One of the most extreme remarks made by a European about the Cherokees in those days was that a Cherokee woman would "take a stick and beat her husband from his head to his heels, and when he could stand it no longer, he would turn over and let her beat the other side."

In 1760, when the great war chief Oconostota had besieged Fort Loudoun and was starving out the English in the fort, he discovered some Cherokee women were smuggling food in to the Englishmen. When he chastised them and threatened them for giving aid to the enemy, the women replied that they had husbands and sweethearts in the fort and that if any harm came to them for what they were doing, their relatives would avenge them. No harm came to them, and they were not stopped.

Finally, we know that the Cherokees at one time had a position of great honor, prestige, and power that was conferred upon a woman. The only woman we know of to hold that position was Nancy Ward, Nanye-hi, known to historians as the Ghigau. Translated variously as Beloved Woman, War Woman, or Red Woman, the word may be a corruption of the Cherokee Giga Agehya, which means literally Red Woman. This title was conferred upon Nanye-hi after she picked up the weapons of her dead husband in a battle with the Creeks and continued fighting. Years later, she married a white man named Brian Ward and became known as Nancy Ward. We do not know the specific powers of the War Woman, or Beloved Woman, except that she had the power to free a captive. She must have had other powers as well.

The matrilineal clan system existed and worked well for many years before white people came to these shores. In my not-so-humble opinion, it was the best family structure that people have ever devised. It was certainly the most secure family for women and children. If a woman tired of her husband for any reason, she could put his belongings out of her house, and that constituted divorce. A mother's brother had the role of teaching and disciplining a male child, so if a father died or was killed or just ran off, no great harm came to the family. If a mother died, her children had as many other mothers as their mother had sisters.

There were no custody battles between divorced parents over their children. Children belonged to their mother's clan, and that was that. If there was spousal abuse, it was abuse of the husband, for no man would mistreat his wife while living in the midst of her clan, surrounded by her brothers and uncles. And if a poor husband was beaten with a stick more than he could stand, he could always take his personal belongings and return to his mother's clan for security.

But all that changed. The change started when white men began living with the Cherokees. In 1690, Cornelius Dougherty came to the Cherokees as a licensed trader. He married and settled down there for the rest of his life. His children bore the surname of Dougherty. Other traders followed. Many of them started Cherokee families. All of them gave their names to their children. This was the beginning of the undermining of the Cherokee clan system.

Donald Day, in his excellent biography of Will Rogers, gives this telling story of an early mixed-blood family: "John Gunther, . . . a mixture of Welsh and English . . . settled in the Cherokee country where . . . he accumulated considerable property." He bartered for the hand of a lovely fifteen-year-old Cherokee girl named Catherine and won her. "When children came, Gunther refused to let her care for them, and when they reached school age sent them to boarding schools. Catherine spoke no English and the children were not allowed to learn Cherokee, so she could not communicate with them."[1] I hope that this Gunther story is atypical, but I fear that it may not be.

By the time of the American Revolution, there were many of these mixed-blood families among the Cherokees: Dougherty, Ward, Pearis, Watts, McDonald, Benge, and others. Even the great war chief Tsiyu Gansini, Dragging Canoe, had a son who was known as Young Dragging Canoe. And when Dragging Canoe led some men out to attack the Watauga settlements, his cousin or sister, Nancy Ward, sent warnings out to the settlers. Some Cherokees were killed as a result of these warnings, and because of this, Nancy Ward has been called a traitor by some writers.

But the facts indicate otherwise. While Dragging Canoe had been talking up the raids, Nancy Ward had been counseling against them. Dragging Canoe ignored her arguments and led the raids anyway. Nancy Ward, in the face of the changing roles of men and women among the Cherokees, was likely standing up for the rights of women. The men should not have gone to war without the approval of the women.

After the American Revolution, the changes continued. In spite of the fact that some people could still trace their lineage entirely through the female line and therefore still knew their clans, they also developed European-style bilateral families and used their father's name as a surname. With the development of the central government of the Cherokee Nation, more of the old clan functions disappeared, being replaced by a legal system patterned after that of the United States. Today, the clans function ceremonially within a small core group of traditionalist, or conservative, Cherokees.

So the old clan system is gone. So what? I believe that to be the worst thing that has happened to Cherokees through the course of history. With all the wars, the diseases, the removal, the lies, and the breaking of treaties, the turning upside down of the family structure has been the most devastating, because it is still with us, and because Cherokee women and children have lost the security that the clan system provided them. Today, many Cherokee families suffer from the same things that other families suffer from: child abuse, wife abuse, custody battles. And there is no end in sight.

There is a saving grace. Even though the clan system has all but disappeared, certain patterns of behavior remain with us. People behave in certain ways because they have always behaved in those ways. They may not remember why they behave that way. It's just the way it is. For example, in some Cherokee families, grown, married children live on the same allotted land their mother lives on. There may be several houses clustered on the allotment. Of course, one reason for that is that the land is free to the children. But it's more than that. Mothers leave home for whatever reason without worrying about their children. If the children want something, they run to an aunt or to their grandmother. It's the old clan system still at work, even though the people involved may not know it.

Cherokee women remain strong and independent. Unless they are victims of some of the horrors outlined above, they still run their families. They still run their homes. They make most of the important decisions. Many are working women who either help their husbands provide for the family or do all of the providing themselves. Many Cherokee women are engaged in tribal politics today. The Cherokee Nation and the Eastern Band of Cherokees have each had one female chief, and other women have run for that high office. A number of women have won seats on the councils of the Cherokee Nation, the Eastern Band, and the United Keetoowah Band.

I have heard some Cherokee men say that women should not be involved in politics, but I believe that attitude is a result of the influence of white men. I for one hope the trend continues. I hope it continues to grow and to strengthen. If we cannot get back the old clan system, and I don't think that is possible, I hope that at least we will arrive at a point where women are indeed, once again, the social and political equals of men. We have come a long way since the day when Nancy Ward said, "You know that women are always looked upon as nothing." We can go even farther.

Henry Starr

I can't help it. Henry Starr is my hero. Henry Starr is the man I would most like to emulate. But times have gotten away from me. There is too much hotshot technology these days. The scale is balanced in favor of the banks as opposed to the honest bank robber. Oh, did I forget? Henry Starr was the greatest bank robber in history. He knew it, too. On his deathbed, he said, "I have robbed more banks than any man in history." And I believe that he had. He had really done it. And that is a hell of an accomplishment. Isn't it?

After all, what are banks? And what are bankers? Just the worst crooks of all time. They want to get our money any way they can. They have created so many ways to get our money away from us that it is unbelievable. They have fees for everything. Over the years, they have foreclosed on more property, they have taken away more things from people, than all the crooks in the world. Their only competitors are insurance salesmen and politicians. And, of course, the corporate sleazes. They are all in league together. I have no sympathy for any of them when they get robbed or when any of them get caught for their nefarious shenanigans.

As happens with so many great people, so many artists, Henry Starr fell into his profession quite by accident. If we can believe his own word. And I do. After all, why would he lie? When he wrote his book, *Thrilling Events*, while in prison, he told things on himself that lead me to believe anything he said. He did not make excuses for anything he did. So why should I not believe him when he told the reasons he had become an outlaw?

Henry Starr was a Cherokee, born near Fort Gibson, Indian Territory (now Oklahoma), in 1873. His was a very prominent old mixed-blood family, with one exceptional branch. James Starr had been killed for being aligned with the Treaty Party. His sons, Tom, Bean, and Ellis, sought revenge, and they went after it in a big way. The Tom Starr legend says that Tom killed one hundred men. That sounds like exaggeration to me. Surely the number is highly inflated. I suspect that the real number is closer to ninety-nine. At any rate, the Cherokee Nation put a price on Tom's head. Eventually, the government forgave him, and old Tom lived to be white-headed and died in bed. But one of his sons, Sam, grew up to be a horse thief and married Myra Belle Shirley, a white woman from Missouri, who was to become famous and notorious as Belle Starr, the Bandit Queen. Belle Starr was killed in 1889. Sam had been killed two years earlier. When his notorious aunt's life was blasted away, Henry was but sixteen years old.

The young man had been born with a reputation, being the son of George "Hop" Starr, Sam's brother and son of the infamous Tom Starr. People expected Henry to be bad. George's health failed, and Henry went to work farming to help feed his family. When his father died in 1886, his mother soon married C. N. Walker, a white man. Henry and his stepfather did not get along at all. In 1888, the family moved to the northern part of the Cherokee Nation, to a place just south of Coffeyville, Kansas. This was cattle country, and soon Henry was working as a cowboy.

In 1891, Henry was falsely accused of stealing two horses. He was arrested and taken to Fort Smith, Arkansas. When his trial came up, the truth came out, and Henry was released, but he had been scarred by the incident. He was ashamed. He felt like a jail-bird, even though he had been innocent. But he learned another lesson from this experience, and it had to do with the corruption of public officials. The deputy marshal who brought him in received $125 for the arrest, $40 for mileage, and $.50 for each meal Henry ate (or was said to have eaten—Henry claimed that he did not get every meal). The man who had falsely accused Henry of the theft and later changed his story at the trial had received $20 for mileage and $1.50 a day while awaiting the trial. Henry believed the whole thing had been arranged between the horse owner and the deputy marshal as a scheme to make money at Henry's expense.

In addition to this treachery, a lawyer (Henry called him a "legal vulture") in Fort Smith, recommended by the deputy marshal, took from Henry $22 and a bill of sale for Henry's horse and saddle. Henry said, "My faith in the majesty of the law and in my fellow man weakened."

Henry went back to work as a cowboy, but one day as he was driving a wagon from Nowata, a man he had known for four or five years asked him to deliver a grip for him. The man was on horseback, so Henry agreed. Along the way, deputy marshals stopped Henry, looked in the grip, and found whiskey, which, of course, was illegal in Indian Territory. Henry was arrested again. He was taken this time to Muskogee, where the federal government had established a "whiskey court." Some friends paid his bond and advised him to plead guilty. He did and was fined $100.

This time, Henry said, his "respect for the law had taken an awful tumble. I began to think that so long as I had the name of being a 'bad one' I might as well have the game." So Henry Starr was driven to a life of crime by corrupt lawmen, unscrupulous citizens, and greedy lawyers. He started out small time but pretty soon graduated to bank robbery, and he was very good at it. He also paid the price, serving several terms in prison. Each time he was a model prisoner. In the course of his bank robberies, no one was ever killed—no one except Henry himself during his last attempt. He did kill one man, a man who started shooting at him on a road without warning and without identifying himself. Henry shot back and killed the man. During one of his stays in prison, he was tried for this killing and condemned to hang.

While he was waiting to be executed, the notorious Cherokee Bill, also in prison waiting to be hanged, got a gun somehow and started shooting up the prison, killing one guard. Henry got the gun away from Bill. Partly because of that and partly because Henry's mother was in Washington, D.C., pleading with the president, Theodore Roosevelt pardoned Henry, and he was set free.

On one occasion, he ran for the office of governor of the state of Oklahoma under an assumed name in an attempt to confuse the voters and help the old train robber Al Jennings win the election. Another time he sent the governor of Oklahoma an irate letter, saying that he was tired of having every crime in the state blamed on him when he had been in Colorado the last several months. The letter was written on stationery from a hotel in Colorado, and the governor's office was in a state of near panic until a secretary noticed that the letter had been postmarked in Tulsa.

During one of his stays in prison, he wrote *Thrilling Events*, detailing his life of crime. Published in 1914 in Tulsa, it sold for fifty cents a copy. The printing job was shoddy, with pages out of order and even paragraphs showing up out of order on pages far apart. He made at least one movie, a reenactment of one of his own bank robberies. It was called *A Debtor to the Law*. Henry said that the movie people robbed him, driving him back to robbing banks.

His criminal career began in 1892 on horseback and ended in 1921 in a Ford car. On his deathbed, he said, "I've robbed more banks than any man in history," and I believe him. He was an artist, even at bank robbing. I think that Henry Starr, if he passed by a bank he had never seen before, even if he had money in his pocket, would not have been able to resist the temptation. He would have said to himself, "I know I can take that bank," and he would have tried. I have admired Henry Starr since I first heard of him years ago.

I admire him for the same reasons that many of us admire Jesse James and the Daltons. Henry was a bank robber, and I think the banks deserve to be robbed. Sometimes I think that if it were not for all the high technology nowadays that has the deck stacked against an honest bank robber, I would rob banks. I admire Henry Starr because he was an artist, not just in his attitude toward banks, but he was a writer and a pretty good one at that. He was an actor. And I admire his philosophy.

Henry Starr was a mixed-blood Cherokee, but he wrote, "I have more white blood than Indian, and with my knowledge of both races, I fervently wish that every drop in my veins was RED." He had seen the times change from the days when the only white people in the Cherokee Nation were renters, "poor white trash who moved from year to year in covered wagons with many dogs and tow-headed kids peeping out from behind every wagon-bow, and who, at the very best, made only a starving crop," to a time when that "same hypocritical renter has grown arrogant and insulting" and the Indian "is an outcast in his own country."

No one told Henry Starr how or what to think. He thought for himself. When it came to religion, Henry Starr was much like Thomas Paine, who said that one man's revelation was hearsay to him. Henry wrote, "I don't believe completely in anything that has or ever will happen; only in the inexorable law of total obliteration and nothingness."

Henry did not blast everyone who was white. He was not a racist. Early in his life he worked for two different white ranchers, and he liked them both. They were good and honest men. He even admired the warden of the last prison he spent time in for having implemented an honor system that, according to Henry, worked. Henry devoted several paragraphs toward the end of *Thrilling Events* to a discussion of the warden's system. He knew his own mind. If he liked or admired something or someone, he let us know, and he let us know why. If he did not like something or someone, he did the same. He spoke his mind. He identified the legitimate crooks, that is, the ones who stole legally, and then he robbed their banks. I think that was wonderful. I admire Henry Starr.

Henry lived and worked in a transitional time period. A time period, in fact, that has been extremely popular in film: *The Wild Bunch*; *Butch Cassidy and the Sundance Kid*; *The Magnificent Seven*; all of the various films about Bonnie and Clyde, Pretty Boy Floyd, and John Dillinger; and, more recently, *The Newton Boys*. The time during which the world moved from riding horseback to driving cars. The time when technology began to outstrip itself. When the cops could call ahead on telephones to set up roadblocks. The time when an honest bank robber no longer had a chance against the overwhelming odds of a combination of modern technology and the law. It's a fascinating period, and Henry Starr lived and carried on his chosen profession throughout the changing times. I often wonder why the filmmakers have ignored him. Could it be because he was Indian?

The final irony of the Henry Starr story is that with all the new technology, he met his end in the good, old-fashioned way. He ordered the teller in the bank to open the safe. The man opened the safe, but he had a gun concealed inside. He picked up the gun, turned, and shot Henry. Henry died a few days later from the gunshot. He was famous in his lifetime. History has shoved him aside in favor of his white aunt-by-marriage, Belle Starr. He worked as a cowboy, he robbed more banks than any man in history, he wrote a book and some newspaper articles, he made movies, he served time in prison and was sentenced to hang but received a presidential pardon. He was a man of his times. Perhaps he was *the* man of the times.

Those times are gone now, along with Henry Starr. I was born at the tail end of those times, in 1940. Though I was unaware of the fact, as a small child I watched those times fade into the modern age. At first the change seemed gradual. We would get something new now and then. Records and record players. Then tapes and tape machines. It didn't seem too diabolical. Then technology just went crazy, and, of course, it all had its application everywhere—in banks, too. Banks are damn near impregnable now, although some fool pulls off a robbery now and then.

I'm getting old now, and more and more I long for the old days. Not the days of my childhood, but older days. I long for the days when a man could rob a bank and hope to get away with it. I long for the days of Henry Starr, and I long for men like Henry Starr. I long to be one of them.

Cherokee Literature

Years ago when I was teaching literature in a state university, I had a textbook for an American literature course that started with a statement that went something like this: "The first American literature was a literature of travel." The author then went on to discuss the writings of people like Captain John Smith and Sir Walter Raleigh. There was no consideration whatsoever that any American Indians had anything like literature. Well, of course they did. We could discuss the controversial claim that the Cherokee writing system is actually an ancient system, and with a writing system, things must have been written down. We could discuss the writing, or near-writing, system of the Mayans. But we don't have to do that. All American Indian tribes had rich and ancient oral literary traditions. Do oral traditions count? Of course. Otherwise, English literature studies would not begin with *Beowulf*. We would not study Homer when we tackle world literature.

Before going further, I should define some terms, well, one term at least: "literature." I know that insurance salesmen and others can be heard to say, "I'll leave you some literature," meaning advertising brochures. Well, let's dismiss that at once. I'm not considering that kind of claptrap as literature, even though one dictionary definition of literature is "anything that is written." This type of "literature" may have been dismissed long ago by Thomas DeQuincy in his essay "The Literature of Knowledge and the Literature of Power," where he uses as an example of the literature of knowledge "a wretched cookery book," and as examples of the literature of power, sermons. Ezra Pound wrote that "literature is language charged with meaning," and "literature is news that stays news." Alexander Solzhenitsyn said that "literature becomes the living memory of a nation."

There have been as many definitions of literature—that is, of "the literature of power"—as there have been people defining literature. Most of us, I believe, think of poetry and fiction and plays when we think of literature, but there is much nonfiction writing as well that fits into all of these grand definitions. And the Cherokee literary tradition has all of these kinds of writing.

It all began with a rich oral tradition, much of which was finally written down for Bureau of American Ethnology publications by James Mooney in the 1890s. Mooney recorded origin tales that explain to us the way the world began and the ways in which various things first came into being. He recorded trickster tales that explore human nature. Jisdu, Rabbit, the Cherokee trickster, can be heroic in one story and cowardly, boastful, or selfish in the next, showing the range of human characteristics. (He was also the model for Br'er Rabbit in the Uncle Remus tales.) There are tales of other animals that also exhibit trickster characteristics. These tales are designed to entertain and to instruct.

And there are stories that are historical: tales of warfare between the Cherokees and various of their ancient enemies and at least one tale detailing a dramatic democratic revolution within Cherokee society. There are fascinating "monster tales," frightening tales of creatures like the *ukitena*, a dragonlike creature that comes from the underworld through waterways; of spear finger, a creature with the appearance of a kindly old grandmother who lures little children to her only to stab them through with her spearlike finger and eat them; of a giant hawk; of a humanlike character with a coat of stone; and many others. Then there is the marvelous collection of doctors' (or medicine men's) recipes, called by Mooney "chants" or "charms." And there are the songs, many of them still in use at Cherokee stomp grounds.

It's a wonderful collection of various kinds of literature, all of them entertaining, instructive, and definitely the "living memory of a nation." Even so, all of this fabulous body of literature, the oral tradition of the Cherokee people, is but the beginning of Cherokee literature, for early in Cherokee history, early in terms of the time of the entry of white people into Cherokee country, Cherokees began writing, in Cherokee and in English. But even before that, white men recorded speeches made by Cherokees, and many of these speeches are certainly worthy of inclusion in the Cherokee literary canon.

One of the earliest of these was a migration tale told to Alexander Long in 1717 by an unnamed Cherokee. It may be a reference to a Bering Strait crossing, and it includes the bringing of corn, peas, pumpkins, and muskmelons. It makes a claim for an ancient writing system that had, by the time of the telling, been lost. Speeches made by Ada-gal'kala (Attacullculla), Oconostota, Dragging Canoe, and Nancy Ward, among others, were recorded. In what is most surely Dragging Canoe's most famous speech, he coined a phrase that has become very well known. It was on the occasion of the signing of the fraudulent Treaty of Sycamore Shoals with the Transylvania Land Company in 1775, when the Cherokee old men sold Kentucky to Hart and Henderson. Dragging Canoe made the following incredibly eloquent and prophetic comments:

> Whole nations have melted away in our presence like balls of snow before the sun and have scarcely left their names behind except as imperfectly recorded by their enemies and destroyers. . . . It was once hoped that your people would not be willing to travel beyond the mountains so far from the ocean on which your commerce was carried and your connections maintained with the nations of Europe. But now that hope has vanished. You have passed the mountains and settled on Cherokee lands. And now you wish to have your usurpations sanctioned by the confirmation of a treaty. When that should be obtained, the same encroaching spirit will lead you onto other lands of the Cherokees. New sessions will be applied for, and finally the country that the Cherokees and our forefathers have so long occupied will be called for, and a small remnant of this nation, once so great and formidable, will be compelled to seek a retreat in some far distant wilderness.

Even there we will dwell but a short space of time before we will again behold the advancing banners of the same greedy host, who, not being able to point out any further retreat for the miserable Cherokees, will then proclaim the extinction of the whole race.

And later that same day, he told the white men, "You have bought a fair land, but you will find its settlement *dark and bloody.*"

The "literature of power" and the "living memory of a nation." Much of Cherokee literature for the following years was in the same category as those memorable words of Dragging Canoe. It was patriotic writing or political writing. When the *Cherokee Phoenix* began publication in the 1820s, with Elias Boudinot as its first editor, much of the writing that appeared in it (in English and in Cherokee) was written in opposition to the clamor for Cherokee removal that was coming from Georgia and from Washington, D.C. Speeches made by Chief John Ross and other prominent Cherokee politicians were also recorded. All of this became part of the great body of Cherokee literature.

But Cherokee literature continued in another vein. Elias Boudinot wrote a novel called *Poor Sarah; or the Indian Woman.* Written and published in Cherokee in 1833, just six years after Sequoyah had presented the Cherokee people with his marvelous syllabary (a system for writing the Cherokee language), it was the first novel written by a Native American and is still one of the very few to be written and published in a Native language.

Twenty-one years later, in 1854, another Cherokee novelist appeared. John Rollin Ridge, son of John Ridge, one of the signers of the infamous Treaty of New Echota (the Cherokee Removal Treaty) who was later killed for his part in that event, published his novel, *The Life and Adventures of Joaquin Murieta, the Celebrated California Bandit.* The novel is a fanciful account of the California bandit Joaquin Murieta. It is entirely the work of Ridge's imagination. In spite of that fact, many writers since have accepted Ridge's novel as history and have built upon it in retelling the tale.

Some have said that Ridge's book should not be considered part of the history of Native American writing, that it is, rather, a novel, written by an Indian, and that it has nothing to do with Indians. I have two responses to that attitude. First, we consider Shakespeare's *Julius Caesar* to be a part of English literature even though it is about ancient Rome. My second response is a little more involved.

When John Rollin Ridge's father was killed, twelve-year-old Rollin and his mother witnessed the bloody event. He later wrote about it: "My mother ran out to him. He raised himself on his elbow and tried to speak, but the blood flowed into his mouth and prevented him. In a few moments more he died, without speaking that last word which he wished to say. Then succeeded a scene of agony the sight of which might make one regret that the human race had ever been created. It has darkened my mind with an eternal Shadow."

Rollin's mother, a white woman, fearing for her own life and the life of her young son, moved to Fayetteville, Arkansas, for safety. She put Rollin in school there. In 1845, she sent him to Massachusetts to finish school. Rollin returned to Arkansas and eventually to the Cherokee Nation, but in 1849 he killed a neighbor, likely in self-defense. But because of the political situation, he moved to Springfield, Missouri, to avoid standing trial. From there he went to California.

During all this time, he had written poetry, much of it with nostalgic Indian themes.

> A thousand cities
> Stand, where once thy nations' wigwam stood,
> And numerous palaces of giant strength
> Are floating down the streams where long ago
> Thy bark was gliding. All is changed.

He wrote articles that were published in newspapers, many of them, according to James W. Parins in his *John Rollin Ridge: His Life and Works*, "advocated that the Cherokees leave their old ways and adapt to the dominant white society."[1] During this time also, Ridge wrote many letters to his uncle, Stand Watie, urging Watie to join with him in organizing an armed attack on the Cherokee government of Principal Chief John Ross, whom Ridge blamed for the killings of the treaty signers.

Upon his arrival in California, Ridge became editor of several California newspapers, he became a prominent California poet, and he wrote his novel. His letters to Stand Watie continued along the same vein, but nothing ever came of them. I speculate, therefore, that his writing about the bandit Joaquin Murieta was one way that Ridge found to cope with his situation. He was a Cherokee in exile, longing to be at home killing the hated enemy. Instead, he wrote about another dark-skinned man who was killing his enemies in California. It was Ridge's vicarious way of doing what he thought he should be doing.

Most of the Cherokee writing that followed, that we know about, was political in nature, although David Brown, a Cherokee, wrote in 1878, a year before he was shot and killed in Muskogee, a poem about Sequoyah. This poem, much like that of Ridge's, though Cherokee in subject matter is classical in style.

> Thou Cadmus of thy race!
> Thou giant of thy age!
> In every heart a place,
> In history a living page;

John Lynch Adair was another newspaper editor and poet. William Trenton Canup, a Cherokee from the Eastern Band, migrated to the Cherokee Nation in the West, where he edited several newspapers in the Cherokee Nation and in Arkansas. He also wrote some short fiction. William Eubanks was a bilingual Cherokee who worked as a translator on various projects and was an essayist. Besides his other writing, he wrote bitter and sarcastic political commentary under the pen name Cornsilk. DeWitt Clinton Duncan was a political writer, a poet, and a fiction writer. Like Eubanks, much of his political writing was done under a pen name, Too qua stee. Other Cherokee writers of the time were Mabel Washbourne Anderson, Ora V. Eddleman Reed, Royal Roger Eubanks, Elias McLeod Landrum, and Rachel Caroline Eaton.[2]

But there are three writers of this period who merit special attention. It's difficult to know just what to say about Will Rogers in a few sentences, he was such a tremendous presence not just on the national scene but on the world scene as well. He was probably the best-known American in the world during his lifetime. He got into show business quite by accident while traveling abroad. His father, Clem, tired of sending money to his spoiled son, cut him off. Will was broke and far away from home. The Texas Jack Wild West Show happened to be traveling in the same part of the world, and Will joined up as a trick roper, using the name The Cherokee Kid. That got him back home. He went on the stage in New York City, working in vaudeville for a time. Eventually, he started talking during his act, saying things that were prompted by newspaper stories. Before long he was starring in movies, writing a syndicated newspaper column, and making after-dinner speeches all over the country. His style was always folksy, down home, and humorous. Before his untimely death in an airplane crash in Alaska in 1935, he had also written several books: *The Illiterate Digest* in 1924, *Letters of a Self-Made Diplomat to His President* in 1926, *There's Not a Bathing-Suit in Russia* in 1927, and *Ether and Me* in 1929. His subjects were usually politics or the U.S. economy or some other topical subject, but much of his writing, in spite of that, remains meaningful to this day.

Will has been accused of being removed from his Cherokee background so much that his writing is scarcely Indian, but that is a false accusation springing from a lack of understanding of things Cherokee or from a careless reading of Rogers's material. Take this comment to a Mayflower group, for example: "My ancestors met yours when they landed. In fact, they would have showed better judgment if they had not let yours land."

A contemporary of Rogers's, and a very successful poet and playwright in his day, was Rollie Lynn Riggs, born in Claremore, Cherokee Nation, in 1899. His poetry often shows Indian themes, and in his plays he wrote about Indian Territory and early Oklahoma and Cherokee characters as well as white ones. Possibly his most Cherokee play is *The Cherokee Night*. His most successful play is *Green Grow the Lilacs*, which was turned into the musical *Oklahoma*.

John Milton Oskison was another contemporary of Will Rogers's, having been a friend and classmate of Will's at Willie Halsell College at Vinita, Indian Territory. While I appreciate all of the above-mentioned writers and the whole oral tradition of Cherokee literature, I feel a closeness to Oskison that I will try to explain in just a little while. From Willie Halsell College, Oskison went to Stanford, where he began writing short stories. He wrote about Indian Territory, about white cowboys, about Indian cowboys, and about Cherokee full-bloods, in stories like "Tookh Steh's Mistake," "Only the Master Shall Praise," and "When the Grass Grew Long," and he met with success early on. His stories were published in *Century Magazine, Overland, Frank Leslie's Monthly,* and *North American Review.*

Oskison graduated from Stanford in 1898 and went to Harvard. After that, he became a newspaper editor and a magazine editor, and later he began writing novels. *Wild Harvest* was published in 1925, *Black Jack Davy* in 1926, and *Brothers Three* in 1935. Critics who have read Oskison's novels, and apparently ignored his short stories, have dismissed him as an Indian writer, saying that he wrote more about white cowboys than about Indians. But when I first read *Black Jack Davy,* I had a strong sense that Oskison would much have preferred writing a novel about Ned Warrior, a full-blood Cherokee character in a minor subplot in the novel, to what he was writing about.

Oskison did write articles on Indian affairs, and he wrote a biography of Tecumseh. He made strong statements on Indian issues in both. And to illustrate further that he was involved in his Cherokee heritage, he wrote a Cherokee novel called *The Singing Bird,* but he was unable to get it published. The manuscript was recently discovered in the Western History Collection at the University of Oklahoma library, and the book has now seen its first publication by the University of Oklahoma Press. Oskison is a major figure in Cherokee literature. He was a groundbreaker. He helped pave the way for all of us.

Today there are a number of Cherokee writers at work: Diane Glancy, Wilma Mankiller, Awiakta, Geary Hobson, Rennard Strickland, Russell Thornton, Daniel Heath Justice, Jace Weaver, Pat Moss,

Julie Moss, Duane Champaign, Robin Coffey, and a number of others to whom I must apologize for having left their names out. Looking back over what I have already written, I notice that I neglected Cherokee historian Emmet Starr and the Cherokee husband and wife team, Jack and Anna Kilpatrick. I'm sure there are more here, too.

One last category of Cherokee writers should be mentioned, and that is the group of Cherokee literary critics. First and foremost among them is Geary Hobson, who is also a poet and a fiction writer. There are the brothers Sean and Chris Teuton. There is Daniel Heath Justice. Finally, Daniel F. Littlefield, Jr., deserves special mention for his incredibly well researched writing on Cherokee history, law, and literature.

I once proposed a course in American Indian literature to the chairman of the English department in which I was teaching, and he said that he doubted if I could find enough material to fill a semester course. I think I could find enough material to fill at least two semester courses on Cherokee literature alone. And I have not mentioned any of the literature written about Cherokees by non-Cherokees.

Cherokee Celebrities

Cherokees have produced an abundance of celebrities. Unfortunately, the list has to start after white people dropped in on us. We have no records of Cherokee celebrities before that, although I am sure that there were some. Perhaps a legendary figure called Dangerous Man could be said to have been a celebrity among the Cherokees. He is said to have led an early migration of Cherokees west, somewhere in or near the Rocky Mountains. No one knows what became of them. They may have become the first Mexican Cherokees, but that is speculation. At any rate, he was so well known that his legend persisted.

Those Cherokees who became well known among the white people as well as their own people during the colonial days were, of course, mostly politicians or warriors, or both. And I suppose the first of these was the man whose name the English wrote down as "Moytoy." His name was most likely Ama-edohi. Sir Alexander Cuming claims to have made "Moytoy" emperor of the Cherokees. The Cherokees, of course, never knew that. But "Emperor Moytoy" became widely known, as far away as England, and there are plenty of living Cherokees today who claim descent from him.

Other Cherokee celebrities include Oconostota, who, among other things, laid siege to Fort Loudoun; Ada-gal'kala (Attacullaculla, or the Little Carpenter), who called himself at one point the president of the Cherokee Nation; and Dragging Canoe (Tsiyu-Gansini), who was so well known and feared by the whites that they bestowed upon him nicknames: the Cherokee Dragon and the Savage Napoleon. His cousin, or sister, Nanyehi, known to historians as Nancy Ward, or the Ghigau, is one of the few early

Cherokee women whose names have been recorded. She is certainly the first female Cherokee celebrity. Like "Moytoy" before her, there are hundreds of contemporary Cherokees who claim to be descended from Nancy Ward.

We can certainly claim celebrity status for Principal Chief John Ross, whose longevity alone would qualify him. He was chief for over thirty years and through some very bad times—the removal, the aftermath of the removal, and the Civil War. Others who became well known during that time were Elias Boudinot, Major Ridge, John Ridge, and Stand Watie, although Watie's real fame came from his military career during the Civil War, when he was the only Indian general in the Confederate army and the last Confederate general to surrender. No other Cherokee politician achieved real fame again until Wilma Mankiller became the first female chief of the Cherokee Nation.

One of the early nonpolitical celebrities among the Cherokees was an outlaw, Henry Starr. He started his outlaw career in the 1890s on horseback and ended it in 1921, having driven a Ford car into town to rob the bank. Like Chief Ross, Henry Starr deserves celebrity status for his career longevity if for nothing else, but he also wrote a book and some articles and acted in movies. When he was returned to Arkansas after having been arrested in Colorado one time, his train was met by a huge crowd, wanting to get a look at the famous outlaw and hoping to hear him speak. Henry, always a crowd pleaser, did give them a show. A man pushed his way through the crowd to stand just below the platform where Henry was in handcuffs and in the company of a U.S. marshal. He said, "I need to talk to that man. I'm sheriff of Benton County, and he robbed my bank." Henry Starr drew himself up and replied, "A man of my reputation and dignity can't afford to be seen in conversation with the sheriff of an ignorant, backwoods Arkansas county."

So far as I know, the first Cherokee professional actor was a man named Frank Boudinot. Frank was, according to S. W. Harman in *Hell on the Border*, a son of the already famous Elias Boudinot. Elias, a brother of Stand Watie, was named Buck Watie at birth. Buck renamed himself after his benefactor, Elias Boudinot, so Boudinot became the family name. Harman says further that Elias

Boudinot and his white wife, Harriet Gould, of Connecticut, had three sons, Frank, Elias Cornelius, and William. Elias was—along with his cousin, John Ridge, and his uncle, Major Ridge—one of the signers of the Treaty of New Echota (the Cherokee Removal Treaty), in 1835, and he was one of the first to be killed for that offense after the removal.

After Elias Boudinot's death in 1839, Stand Watie sent Harriet and the children north for their safety. Growing up in the North, Frank Boudinot never returned to the Cherokee Nation. He became an actor, using the stage name of Frank Starr. When the Civil War broke out, Frank enlisted in the Union army. He rose to the rank of a commissioned officer, but he was wounded in one of the last battles of the war, later dying from the wound. His wife, named Brinsmaid, was an actress, and their son, who also used the name Frank Starr, was for a time an actor. He died in the 1890s in New York City.

From there we jump to the 1930s when Victor Daniels, from Muskogee, a full-blood Cherokee, became the first film Tonto in the Lone Ranger series to Bob Livingston's Lone Ranger. Daniels used the professional name of Chief Thundercloud. He also played Geronimo in the 1939 film of the same name. He was in dozens of other movies, sometimes playing villainous Indians, sometimes sympathetic ones.

Monte Blue was a mixed-blood Cherokee who started acting in silent films and finished in talkies in the 1950s. He had been a star in his earlier movies, but he retired and went abroad. While enjoying his retirement, his finances suffered from the stock market crash, and he was forced to return to acting. The break of a few years, however, caused a change in his career. In his last years, he played in mostly B pictures, including a good many westerns. He might show up as a white man, usually a villain, or as an Indian. Interestingly enough, he played the principal chief of the Cherokee Nation in a 1949 Monte Hale western, *Ranger of Cherokee Strip*. Though the characters are all fictional, as is the plot, the movie is interesting in that it comes close to depicting the Cherokee Nation as it really was in pre-Oklahoma days. Blue's "Chief Hunter" appears in a long-tailed black suit in his office.

Many western movie stars have claimed to have Cherokee blood, including Tom Mix, but of course almost everything in the world was claimed for Mix in his publicity, so we can take that one with a grain of salt. Walter Brennan, Jack Hoxie, Glenn Strange, Iron Eyes Cody, Ben Johnson, Burt Reynolds, James Garner, and many others are in this category.

Others have definite connections to one of the three federally recognized Cherokee tribes. Carl "Cherokee" Matthews had a long career as a villain in B western movies. Although he lived in Los Angeles, he remained active in Cherokee causes back home in the Cherokee Nation.

One of my favorite Cherokee actors since I was a young teenager in the 1950s has been Clu Gulager. I remember I was watching an episode of a new western series on television called *The Tall Man*, which starred Clu Gulager as Billy the Kid and Barry Sullivan as Pat Garrett. My father came into the room and said, "You know, Clu is Cherokee from up home." I already liked him, but after that, I liked him even better. Much later I got to know Clu personally, and I feel privileged to be able to call him a friend. Another friend of Clu's was Dennis Weaver, also a Cherokee Nation tribal member. Clu has never, to my knowledge, played an Indian character in a film. Dennis Weaver has, but he should not have. He looked ludicrous.

A local Cherokee who worked for the Cherokee Nation at the same time I did back in 1976 disappeared from Tahlequah for a few years and then reappeared on the national scene. Wes Studi came on the movie screens strong a few years ago with powerful performances in *Dances With Wolves*, *The Last of the Mohicans*, and *Geronimo*, that latter making him the second Cherokee to play Geronimo, an Apache. Wes has also taken on roles that are not written for Indian actors, giving his career a longer lasting quality.

Joe Thornton was the 1970 U.S. archery champion.

Gene Conley played both professional basketball and professional baseball. When I was about thirteen years old, my grandmother gave me a Gene Conley baseball card and told me that we were related somehow. I never met Gene, but I have corresponded with him and his wife and have talked with Gene on the telephone.

As far as I know, Gene is the only professional athlete to have championship rings from two different professional sports. He played for the Boston Celtics when they won three consecutive NBA world championships, 1959–1961, and he pitched for the 1957 Milwaukee Braves when they won the World Series.

And although his professional career was somewhat disappointing, Sonny Sixkiller was a star college football quarterback for the University of Washington in 1970, his photograph appearing on the cover of *Sports Illustrated*.

We have a Cherokee opera singer, Barbara McAlistir, and pop singers Keely Smith and Rita Coolidge.

Will Rogers may have been the most popular Cherokee celebrity of all time. He was first known as a trick roper in a Wild West show, then in vaudeville. He then added talk to his rope act and became very popular. He would usually talk about topical subjects, often beginning with, "All I know is just what I read in the papers." Soon he was starring in major motion pictures like *Judge Priest* and *A Connecticut Yankee in King Arthur's Court*, and he was writing a widely syndicated newspaper column. He was much in demand as a speaker, and he produced a few books. When he died in an airplane crash in Alaska in 1935, the whole world mourned.

But the absolute first major Cherokee celebrity was Sequoyah. After suffering years of ridicule and abuse for spending all his time trying to develop a writing system for the Cherokee people, Sequoyah finally did it. He presented his syllabary to the Cherokees in 1821, and it was widely, I should say, universally accepted. It has been said that the Cherokee Nation "became literate overnight," surely a slight exaggeration. The *Cherokee Phoenix* began publication in 1828 in Cherokee and in English. News of Sequoyah's remarkable accomplishment spread rapidly. He was hailed as the "Cherokee Cadmus." When he went to Washington as part of a delegation from the Western Cherokees, he was wined and dined and interviewed. He apparently found all of the attention from white folks to be distasteful. He told one interviewer, through an interpreter, for he could speak no English, that he had five wives and twenty children and that he had created the syllabary by listening to the sounds of birds and animals in the wilderness. It was his little joke, and it worked, for the writer took it seriously, and so have a number of writers afterward. When Sequoyah finally left the Cherokee Nation for Mexico and died there, the Cherokee Nation sent a search party to look for him. The Cherokee Nation had caused a medal to be struck for Sequoyah for his great accomplishment, and he was awarded a pension, which his widow continued to collect after his death. He was a great man and an early Cherokee celebrity, not just among the Cherokees, but nationally and even worldwide.

I would add a paragraph on Cherokee writers (there are a number of them), but I once heard a writer say to another writer, "You know, at best we writers are minor celebrities." He was right, of course. How many times have you heard someone say something like, "I read a great book the other day," and you have asked, "Who wrote it?" The response was something like, "Gee. I can't remember." In spite of all that, I would be tempted to write something here about the many Cherokee writers, but for the life of me, I can't remember their names.

Indian Humor

I can't find my copy of Washington Irving's *Tour of the Prairies*, but I can recall the gist of something he wrote in it. He said that when his bunch camped for the night, the white men sat around one fire, and the Indians with them sat around another fire some distance away. He said that white people had an image of the Indians as a stoic, somber people, but he said that this was decidedly not true. At night, among themselves, around their own campfire, he said the Indians talked and laughed all through the night. He supposed that when Indians were around white people, they just did not find much to laugh about.

If any writers ever read *Tour of the Prairies*, they either skipped this part, or forgot it, or deliberately ignored it, or perhaps they thought that Irving just made it up. I can't recall another white writer for years after Irving ever writing anything that even hinted that Indians might have a sense of humor. We do, of course, and always have had.

In 1824, a group of Cherokees was in Washington to negotiate with the government on the Georgia Compact, which called for the total removal of all eastern Indians. A congressman from Georgia on the floor of the House of Representatives called the Cherokees "savages subsisting upon roots, wild herbs, disgusting reptiles." Later, George Lowrey, full-blood Cherokee, found himself sitting across the table from that same man at dinner. A waiter was passing by with a dish of sweet potatoes. Lowrey demanded "some of those roots," explaining, still in a loud voice, that "we Indians are very fond of roots."

When Sequoyah was being interviewed in Washington in 1828 by a Mr. Knapp, he was apparently tiring of all the attention.

Knapp asked him how he came to distinguish all the sounds in the Cherokee language. "I listened to the sounds of the birds and the animals in the forest," Sequoyah said. When Knapp asked him about his family, Sequoyah responded, "I have five wives and twenty children, and I cannot recall all their names." White people, who never read Washington Irving, have repeated those responses as factual.

I find it very interesting that while white people have not seen in Indians a sense of humor, they have praised Will Rogers to high heaven for being a humorist. And they made him rich, paying to see him on stage, or in the movies, or buying his books, or reading his column in the newspaper. He told them often enough that he was Cherokee. I guess they just failed to take it seriously.

Henry Starr, the famous bank robber, was being a humorist when he decided to try to help the old train robber Al Jennings win the office of governor of Oklahoma. He said that he thought Jennings should win because all politicians were crooks, but Jennings had paid for his crimes. The others had not. So Henry went downtown and filed to run for governor under an assumed name that was very close to that of the incumbent, hoping to confuse the voters.

On another occasion, when the governor of Oklahoma put a price on Henry's head, Henry wrote him an indignant letter claiming to have been in Colorado for several months and accusing the governor of blaming every crime in Oklahoma on him. The letter was written on stationery from a hotel in Colorado. The governor's office was in a tizzy until a secretary noticed that the letter had been postmarked in Tulsa.

Humorous remarks or funny statements or even jokes told by Indians have gone right over the heads of white people for years, probably because those white people already knew that Indians had no sense of humor. Therefore, they figured, the remark wasn't really funny. They misunderstood it. But sometimes Indian humor is different in kind from white people's humor. I have heard the following joke told or have told it myself on several different occasions, and each time, white people have not thought it funny while Indians have laughed, sometimes to the point of nearly falling out of their chairs: There was a Texan who took an Indian for a ride in his car, and when they got well out into the wide open Texas landscape, the Texan stopped the car, and they got out. The Texan swept his arms out and said, "Just look at all that. Look at it. As far as you can see in any direction, that's all my land. Why, it takes me all day to drive across my land." The Indian looked and said, "Hmph. I used to have a pickup like that."

I had a very good friend, now deceased, who was a full-blood Cherokee who had been born in Texas. His father was working down there. The father was a big fan of Texas politician W. Lee "Pappy" O'Daniel, so when his son was born, he named him W. Lee O'Daniel Robbins. Now, that in itself is Indian humor at its best—or perhaps its worst. W. Lee O'Daniel Robbins was called Dan until I met him, and he told me the story of his full name. I started calling him W. Lee, and soon the rest of our acquaintances were calling him that too. W. Lee decided to try to sell one of my novels to a Hollywood producer, and he had been talking to this producer for some time. He called the office one day, and the man who answered the phone told him that the producer was out. "Who is calling?" the man asked, and when W. Lee identified himself, the man on the other end of the line said, "Oh! Mr. W.!" When I heard that story, I changed his name again, and everyone else followed my lead and called him Mr. W. We had visions of people in the film business in Hollywood talking to one another about the mysterious Mr. W.

Mr. W. had a wicked sense of humor. One Thanksgiving when his boys were small, he told them not to run through the kitchen as he was cooking a turkey, and if they ran in the house, especially in the kitchen, they would cause the turkey to fall. Sure enough, the boys ran through the kitchen. Mr. W. yelled at them. He opened the oven door and said, "Look what you did." In the oven was a Cornish game hen he had obviously put there just for this purpose.

Mr. W. suffered from diabetes, and toward the end of his life began losing appendages. The forefinger on his right hand was cut off. He told us that he had a funeral for it and one hundred women showed up.

A Cherokee medicine man who is a friend of mine told me once that some of his Mexican clients had told him how cheaply he could live in Mexico, and he was considering making the move. "You can live practically like a king on next to nothing," he said. "You can have a maid and everything, and for just a few dollars more each month, she'll even wash your feet. I'm thinking about moving down there, because I can't hardly reach my feet any more."

I was in a peyote meeting on the Crow Reservation in Montana one time. The Road Man was Barney Old Coyote. In the middle of the night, we took a break and went into the house to drink coffee, smoke, and talk. Barney started explaining to me the importance of names to Crow people. He told me about a famous Crow from years earlier who was known for his generosity. He gave everything he had away to others. When he had given away all his belongings, he even gave his wife to another man. Then with nothing left in the whole world, he walked out into the center of the village one day, standing naked, threw his arms up in the air, and shouted, "I throw myself away." That became the man's name. He Throws Himself Away. Barney went on to explain what a great man he was. He was an example to everyone. Then he gestured to one of his nephews. "This boy has the same name now," he said. Everyone was sitting solemnly and respectfully around the table, and Barney added, "These guys call him Garbage Can."

When I went to Sioux City, Iowa, as director of the Indian Studies Program at Morningside College, Felix White, Sr., a Winnebago, became a very good friend. He came in from the Winnebago Reservation to meet me when I first arrived. He was always willing to show up to speak to a class. One day he walked into my office and sat down without saying a word. He sat slumped over and wearing a very long expression on his seventy-year-old face. At last he spoke. "Three old timers died out at Winnebago this week," he said. "They usually go in fours. I'm going to be real careful, because I don't want to go *with that bunch.*"

Sometimes the humor is accidental, especially when it comes from a small child. When my oldest granddaughter was still in Cherokee Nation Head Start, she was a part of a small choir that on some special occasion, which I had to miss, sang, among other songs, "Frere Jacques," not in French, but in Cherokee and in English. When I saw her next, I said, "I heard that you sang "Brother John," and she said, "Yeah. In Cherokee and in, uh, just plain."

Two categories of Indian humor would make Indians mad if they were told by white folks, but Indians love to tell them on themselves. They are drunk jokes and jokes about Indians speaking broken English. I know of one in each category that was told on the same man, a Cherokee, who will remain nameless here. One fellow said of him, "He's the only Indian I know whose only language is English, and he still talks broken English." And it was said, "He drove into downtown Tahlequah drunk the other night. The only other car on the road was parked, and he still hit it."

Some Indian students at Morningside College were sitting around the Indian student lounge talking one day. One of them told this tale about some Indians at Haskell Institute in Lawrence, Kansas. Some Indian boys were cruising around one day, and they spotted some Indian girls walking down the sidewalk. "Get in," they said. The girls refused. "Aw, come on," the boys said. One of the girls said, "No. We won't get in. You might something us." One of the boys answered, "No. Come on. We won't nothing you."

I was talking on the phone to my good friend Richard King, Assiniboine, one day while I was in Sioux City. He had just given me the news about his new job and about the new job of our mutual friend, Kenny Ryan, also Assiniboine. I said, "Richard, what's the world coming to? Here I am, director of Indian Studies, and you're a tribal judge, and Kenny is tribal chairman. I don't know what to make of all that." Richard said, "Oh, well, at least none of us works for the Bureau."

Richard came down to Tahlequah from Montana once to visit me. He left the house in the evening and drove off somewhere. When he came back the next morning, I asked him where he had been. "Oh," he said, "out counting Baptist churches."

Richard was in a crowd of Indians and one white girl in my Indian studies office one day when the subject of Indians eating dogs came up somehow. The white girl said, "Indians eat dogs? Euh." Richard replied, "Well, white people eat chickens. Euh."

Someone once asked a Cherokee from North Carolina how come the Cherokee clans are matrilineal. His answer was full of wisdom. "My wife had five kids," he said. "She tells me they're all mine."

Indians have been moved about so much by the U.S. government, but have found their way back home somehow, that a standard line back when the space program was still new used to be, "If they're worried about how to get those astronauts back safely, they ought to send an Indian out there. He'd find his way home." Indian casinos are now the subject of much of Indian humor. One wag said, "I've lost so much money in those damn casinos that now all I do is drive through the parking lot, roll down my window and toss my money out." I have a cousin who calls them toilets because that's where you flush all your money away.

I have a brother-in-law named Charles Snell, but everyone calls him Chug. In his younger days, he ran around quite a bit. In those days, he lived in a mobile home on a hill beside his mother's home on their allotment. At the bottom of the hill was an apple orchard. Someone was telling a story on Chug one day. They said that he arrived home one time about three o'clock in the morning, and as he crawled out of his pickup, his wife appeared in the doorway of the house with a shotgun. KA-BOOM went the shotgun. Chug dived headlong down the hillside. When everyone had finally quit laughing, Chug said, "Yeah. Many's the morning I've had apples for breakfast."

Chug's a construction worker. He was doing a job on a high school one time, and he found some discarded tall band hats in the dumpster. He dug out enough for all his kids and took them home. Then he put a hat on each of the five kids and had them march around in the yard. When he was cleaning up his yard on another occasion, he had all of the kids lined up from the tallest to the shortest, each carrying something—the smallest in the rear had only a piece of paper—marching single file to the private dump a short distance away.

Chug's wife is a white woman. He calls her a hillbilly. After a hard rain, there was a big puddle in front of his mother's house. They drove up to the puddle and got out of the car. Chug had his wife carry him across the puddle. She picked him up like a baby and splashed right through the muddy water.

Indian women are notorious for being overly cooperative if they're in an office or someplace that has a white man in charge of things. Here's a joke that an Indian woman friend of my wife sent her by e-mail the other day.

> An Indian woman took a baby to the hospital for its checkup. The doctor looked the baby over, and then he asked the woman, "Is he bottle or breast fed?"
>
> The woman answered, "He's breast fed." So the doc said, "All right, strip to the waist."
>
> The woman did, and the doc pinched her nipples.
>
> "Well," he said. "I see the problem. You don't have any milk." The woman looked at the doctor and said, "I'm his grandma."

There's an Indian T-shirt that has the following lettered on it: "I'm part white but I can't prove it."

I have seen something written about Indian humor only twice (not counting the brief mention by Washington Irving). The first was in a magazine back in the 1970s. I'm pretty sure it was written by a white man, and it was decidedly academic and unfunny. The second was a chapter in Vine Deloria Jr.'s *Custer Died for Your Sins*. It's title, I believe, was "Indian Humor." It was far more interesting and meaningful than was the white man's study. In that chapter, Deloria told a joke on Cherokees that I should repeat here for the sake of fairness to all sides. (I've lost my copy of *Custer Died for Your Sins*, too, so this is paraphrased.)

> There was a prosperous Cherokee farmer who hired a white man to help around the place. He caught the white man smoking in the barn one day and told him not to do that. It was too dangerous. One day the Cherokee told the white man that he had to go to town to run some errands. "And don't be smoking in the barn," he said just before he left. When the Cherokee came home several hours later, he found his barn and his house burned down, his wife raped, and his cow killed. This made him mad as hell. He started tracking that white man. He tracked him out of Oklahoma and across Kansas into Colorado. He went through Nebraska, Wyoming,

Montana, and into Canada. At last he found himself in Alaska out in the boonies. The trail led him to a lone shack. There was deep snow all around, and smoke was coming out of the chimney of the little place. The Cherokee walked closer, and then he saw the white man sitting in front of the shack smoking a pipe. The Cherokee said, "Are you the man who burned my barn and house and raped my wife and killed my cow?" The white man puffed his pipe and said, "Yeah. What of it?"

The Cherokee gave the white man a hard look and said, "You better watch that shit."

The interesting thing about this joke is that it's almost a capsule of Cherokee history since nearly the end of the American Revolution, the time when Cherokees stopped fighting the United States. The federal government kept taking and kept pushing, and the Cherokees sometimes protested, but in the end, they took it. And that's what this joke is about. Humor is often a disguise for the profound.

I could write on and on telling jokes, humorous anecdotes, and funny stories, but I fear I have reached the point with this where I will be expected to say something profound about the subject, or if I can't quite manage that, at least to do some speculating about or say something analytical about the subject of Indian humor. I can think of some things that have been said and probably will be said again, but I don't want to say them. I think the truth of the matter is just that Indians are smart, have tremendous senses of humor, and really like to laugh. I think that's all that really needs to be said.

The Five Civilized Tribes

In the 1820s, the Cherokees undertook a plan of voluntary assimilation in an effort to make their white neighbors in the Southern states willing to keep them on as neighbors. There was a tremendous effort on the part of the Southern whites to have all Indians removed from their homes east of the Mississippi River to locations out west. Because of the charged language of the times, some Cherokees thought that the "civilized" whites simply objected to "savages" living in the vicinity. They decided that if they overhauled their society and made it look more like that of the white people, white people would no longer have objections. So they set about the task with a vengeance.

They built schools and hired white teachers from Northern schools to come down to the Cherokee Nation and teach their children. They invited missionaries to their country and provided land for the missions, which also had schools connected to them. The wealthier Cherokees, mostly but not all mixed-bloods, built homes like those of the wealthy Southern plantation owners. They themselves then became owners of plantations and raised cotton crops with slave labor. They divided their country into voting districts and held elections. They wrote and adopted a new constitution, based largely on that of the United States. They began making the transition from the old clan law to the new written law, and organized a complete legal system, with written laws, law enforcement officers, and courts.

During this time, Sequoyah presented the Cherokees with a syllabary, a system for reading and writing in the Cherokee language. The Cherokee Nation had type made and bought a printing press.

The constitution and laws were printed in the Cherokee language and in English. They began publishing a bilingual newspaper, the first in the United States. Elias Boudinot, the first editor of the *Cherokee Phoenix*, wrote a novel that was published in Cherokee.

This whole movement had begun naturally, even before the deliberate efforts began, as a result of the large number of mixed-blood Cherokee families in the Cherokee Nation. Some Cherokee families were taking on characteristics of European families, using the father's surname as a family name, having the father as head of the household, forgetting the old clan affiliations. Many, if not most, had become Christian, and they took to heart the anti-feminist writing of Paul. The New Testament was translated into the Cherokee language and published in Cherokee.

The Choctaws, Chickasaws, Creeks, and Seminoles followed the Cherokee example, and they all did so well in this monumental effort that they became known as the Five Civilized Tribes, a label that has stuck to this day. The first thing the Cherokees and the other four tribes learned about being "civilized" was that it did not make a damn bit of difference to the Southerners, from the governor down to the poorest whites. They wanted the Indians' land, and that was that. But I am not here writing about the greedy whites, the almost unbelievable Georgia anti-Cherokee laws, or even about the horrors of the removal. I'm more interested right now in semantics.

Cherokees, more than the other four tribes, have suffered much ribbing from Indians of other tribes about being called "civilized." I assume that this comes from the perceived insult to them by the use of the term. In other words, if Cherokees, Choctaws, Chickasaws, Creeks, and Seminoles are the Five *Civilized* Tribes, what does that make all the other tribes? According to Francis Jennings in *The Invasion of America*, the words "civilization" and "savagery" have no meaning whatever if taken as absolutes, other than that one is seen to be the opposite of the other. Therefore, if Cherokees and the other four tribes are the "civilized" tribes, then all of the others are, by implication, still "savage." Other Indians, I think quite naturally, resent the Five Civilized Tribes label, and I think the members of the five tribes are beginning to resent it as well.

Why is that? It's not that we Cherokees are not proud of all the accomplishments that our people made in the days before the removal and the days following. We are proud that the Cherokee Nation built the first institution of higher education west of the Mississippi River, installed the first telephone west of the Mississippi, and accomplished many other things. But that does not mean that we are ashamed of our ancestors who came before that. It does not mean that we are ashamed of our own ancient civilization.

And when they call us one of the Five Civilized Tribes, they are not just implying, they are stating emphatically that Cherokee society, before it began imitating the white people's society, was not civilized. It was, of course. It had its own civilization. It had its art, its music, its religion, its government, its literature, its social and family structures, its methods of child rearing and education, its view of the universe, its medicine, and its games, and in spite of later treaty language, the Cherokees had long been farmers. Some of this ancient civilization is still with us, in spite of history. It mostly resides at the stomp grounds, where the old religion is practiced, and with Cherokee medicine people who carry on old ways.

I am proud of what is left of that ancient civilization, as I am proud of all of the accomplishments that came after. I don't want only one phase of that long history of Cherokee civilization to be called civilized. I don't believe that any one people should be called civilized over another, and I don't believe that any one period of anyone's history should be called civilized as opposed to any other period. Civilization is the grand total of any people's lifeways. It's that simple. "Civilization" and "savagery" have become words like "squaw," and "papoose" and "warrior" and "brave" and "tribe" and "tribal member." They are words that are most often used casually with little or no thought given as to what they really mean. They are words that should not be used, unless they are used carefully and properly.

Cherokees are a civilized people. Cherokees have always been a civilized people. So have all of the Indian people of the Americas, and all of the people of the world. We have all developed our different civilizations, civilizations that worked for us in our environments. Things have happened throughout the course of history to alter those civilizations, but no one has become more or less civilized as a result of those changes. So let's stop talking nonsense and say to hell with that "civilized" tribe label. What do you say?

Cherokee Names

My understanding of Cherokee naming in the old days (read that, in the days before the influence of the white man was widespread) is that an old woman in the clan would be asked to name the newborn child. Names were clan names, so that the old woman would have a choice of old clan names that were no longer in use, that is, names that belonged to people who had died. The names of the dead were not to be spoken until they were given anew. Just how or why the old woman chose the name she did, I do not know. I do believe, however, that a person did not use his or her real name. If one knew another's name, it would be much easier and more effective to make bad medicine against that person. So nicknames were widespread. I should say, common. Nicknames could be given for just about any reason.

Some of them are comical, obviously teasing names. On one of the old rolls I saw a Wrinkle Sides and a Wrinkle Butt. When white men wrote down Cherokee names, they were likely either writing down nicknames or titles, not names given at birth. Stalking Turkey could be one of those nicknames, making reference to the way a man walked, or it could be a shortened form of a name like "He Is Stalking the Turkey." Cherokee names are often, when translated into English, complete sentences.

There are chants, or charms, used to aid a woman in giving birth. One form calls a boy out, another calls a girl. If a boy, he is called "Ballsticks," if a girl, "Sifter." After birth, a boy or a girl might just be called "Usdi," a word meaning either "little" or "baby." Later in life a boy would likely just be called "Boy," in Cherokee, "Achuja," short form, "Chuj." Lots of Cherokee boys still today go through life known only as "Chuj." I don't know of a similar nickname for a girl, but there may be one. However, "Guwisti," meaning "sifter" or "sieve," is a girl's given name. It is, in fact, my wife's Cherokee name.

The common practice these days is, for the more or less traditional people, to give a child an English name and a Cherokee name. My wife, Evelyn Snell (Conley), is Guwisti. Her father's names were Swimmer Wesley Snell and Adawosgi. Adawosgi, in Cherokee, means "he is swimming." Translated into English, it is changed to "Swimmer," because using a sentence for a name in English sounds too weird. It is interesting that the translation of his Cherokee name was his first name in English. As a small child, Evelyn always called him Adawosg'. The family name, Snell, is also interesting. It comes from the Cherokee "Elaqui," meaning "snail." About three generations back, in Evelyn's family line, the name was Anglicized to "Snell." There are still branches of the family that use Snail for their last name.

Swimmer is an interesting case in itself. There are lots of Cherokees named Swimmer. It is a first name and a last name. Actually, it is two completely different names. Adawosgi means "he is swimming (the way a man swims)," or "he is bathing." Put into English it becomes simply "Swimmer." Ayunini means "he is swimming (like a snake)." In English, it is also just "Swimmer."

An English version, or equivalent, of the nickname "Chuj" is "Sonny." Almost every Cherokee family has a Sonny. I have said that if one were to go downtown in Tahlequah and stand on Muskogee Avenue (the main street) and yell out, "Sonny," about a dozen Cherokee boys would look around.

I don't have a Cherokee name. I wish I did. A friend of mine from Laguna Pueblo told me once that I could give myself a name, but I wouldn't feel right about that. I did have an agent once who suggested that if I gave myself a "more Indian sounding name," I might sell more books. I said to her, "What do you want me to call myself? Blue Feather Up His Ass?" I do have, however, a name that made its way into the Cherokee language early in history in two different forms. Apparently, when Cherokees first met a white man named Robert, they tried to say his name, and because the Cherokee language has no R and no B, it came out as

Gwagwa, or Gwag, or at a different time and place, as Lawun. Both forms have become standard in the language.

There are other foreign names that have made their way into the Cherokee language. George is Jaji. Charles is Tsali. Betty is Gwedi. Mary is Meli. Ann is an easy one—it's Ana. John is Tsan. And so on.

A lot has happened to Cherokee naming, or, rather, nicknaming practices over the years. Going back to the American Revolution, we can look at a few names and a few processes. A prominent Cherokee politician was known as Ada Gal'kala (written down by English-men as Attacullaculla), translated into English as "The Leaning Wood." I have no idea of the significance of that name. But when the white people saw that he was skillful at "crafting a deal," they nick-named him "The Little Carpenter." His son (most historians say) was named (or nicknamed?) Tsiyu Gan'sini, meaning literally, "he is dragging the canoe," but called in English, Dragging Canoe. The story behind this name is interesting and informative.

His father (more likely his maternal uncle) was going on a raid with some other men, and the boy wanted to go along. He was told, "You're too small. Stay home." The boy insisted. He kept fol-lowing the men, and they kept telling him to go home. At last he hid in the woods and still followed along. The men got to the river, where they began putting their huge dugout war canoes into the water. It took a few men to lift one of them. The father (uncle) looked back and saw the boy still lurking around, still longing to go to war with the men, so he finally said, "All right. Put your boat into the water and come along." After that, the men went on about their business, until one happened to notice the boy again. "Look!" the man called out. "He is dragging the canoe." That, or a version of that, became the boy's name, and he kept it all of his life.

His female cousin was known as Nan'yehi, until she went to battle with her husband against the Creeks. Her husband was killed in the battle, and she picked up his weapons and continued the fight. For that reason, she was officially given the title War Woman. White historians wrote it down as "the Ghigau." That's likely a cor-ruption of the Cherokee words "Giga Agehyuh," meaning "red" and "woman," and from then on she was only called War Woman or the Ghigau. Later, she married a white man named Ward and became known as Nancy Ward.

When men or women had earned titles, they used those as names, and since each Cherokee town had men with the same titles, it was once common, for example, to speak of the Mankiller of Hiwassee, or the Mankiller of Chota, or of whatever other town. Many of these earned titles became surnames in English. There were a number of "killer" titles, and so surnames. Today there are Mankillers, Fivekillers, Sixkillers, Tenkillers, Pathkillers. There used to be Choctawkillers, Chickasawkillers, Womankillers, and Niggerkillers. Some of them dropped the first part of their name to become just Killers. And then there are Tehees. (Tehee is Cherokee for killer.) We can assume all these "killer" names to have originally been earned as war names or titles. As Hudson says in *The Southeastern Indians*, "One of the main preoccupations of Southeastern Indian men was the acquisition of war names and titles."[1]

There are descendants of Dragging Canoe who have used their Cherokee name and then shortened and Anglicized it to become Conseens. (From the second word, the "dragging" in Dragging Canoe's name, Tsiyu Gansini.) There are also people with the last name "Canoe."

Some names or nicknames came about simply as a result of sound. A Cherokee with the English surname of Benge became known as the Bench. Diwali, whose Cherokee name meant either bowl or mushroom, maybe both, became known as Bowl or the Bowl or even Bowles. Both of these men were associated with Dragging Canoe. And there was Tahchee, who was known in English as Captain Dutch. The sound association is obvious, but I have no idea which came first, the Dutch or the Tahchee.

John Stuart was a white man, a Scot with red hair, who was the British superintendent of Southern Indian Affairs. He married a Cherokee woman and lived among the Cherokees. They nicknamed him Bushyhead, and that became the family name of his descendants.

When he became a Christian, a Cherokee named Oowatie, or the Old One, Anglicized his name to Watie and used it as a surname. He took the two names Christian and David to put in front of it.

He had two sons who became prominent Cherokees. Buck Watie, his oldest son, went to college, where he had a benefactor named Elias Boudinot. Buck took his name in his honor. His children were Boudinots. His brother was Isaac S. Watie, later famous as General Stand Watie. "Stand" was shortened from the translation of his Cherokee name Degataga, meaning "two people are standing close together."

Sequoyah's name is a mystery. We have no idea what it means or even what language it is in. It has been said to translate into English as "The Lame One" and "Pig's Place." The Lame One makes no sense whatever, and to make Sequoyah into Pig's Place we would have to change the spelling of the first part to "Sikwa" and change the final syllable from "yah" to "yi." I have never seen the following proposed except in my own writing, but I would suggest this possibility. The first part of the name is "Sikwa." Sikwa means "pig" in contemporary Cherokee. However, sikwa originally meant opossum. When Cherokees acquired pigs from white men, they thought that the animals bore a resemblance to opossums, so they called them by that name. Then to distinguish between the two, they called the opossum "sikwa-ujetsdi," meaning the grinning sikwa. But "ya" or "yah" is an intensive and is often translated as "real" or "original," as in "yunwiya," meaning "real person," or "tsisqua-ya" (sparrow), meaning "real bird." So what happens if we put the intensive on the end of "sikwa"? We come up with "Sikwa-ya" (Sequoyah?). Or the "real sikwa," or more to the point, the "original sikwa," or the 'possum.

A Cherokee man known as Gal'kaliski was fighting with Andrew Jackson's forces at the Battle of Horseshoe Bend. It has been said that General Jackson was down and about to be done in by a Creek. Gal'kaliski stepped in just in time to save the general's life. After the battle was over and won by Jackson's forces, with much help from the Cherokees, Jackson told Gal'kaliski that they would be friends forever, that as long as he lived, "the Cherokees' feet would be pointed East." When Jackson became president and the agitation from the Southern states for Cherokee removal, particularly from Georgia, was getting fierce, and Jackson seemed to be behind Georgia, Gal'kaliski told the people that he would go to Washington and talk to Jackson. He was certain that Jackson would not forget the man who had saved his life. He made the trip, but Jackson would not let him in. Jackson would not see him. Gal'kaliski said, "*Detsinu lahungu*," meaning, "I tried, but I failed." Thereafter he was called Tsunu lahunski, "He Tried but Failed." The name was Anglicized into Junaluska.

The more conservative Cherokees today still have an English name and a Cherokee name, and many of them have nicknames as well. Cherokees love to use nicknames. Although I do not have a Cherokee name, I have had a nickname. Because my middle name is Jackson, my grandfather called me Stony, for Stonewall Jackson. When my younger brother came along, Grandpa called him Little Rock. Cherokees also, often because of divorce and remarriage of parents, take on different last names. I know a guy who used to call himself James Grass but later was going by James McIntosh.

My brother-in-law, whose name is Charles, is known far and wide as Chug. I'm sure that he has a Cherokee name as well, but I don't know it. He has children, Bubby, Sissy, Lunkhead or Lunky, Gassy, and Meathead or Meat. I still don't know all their real names. When Gene LeRoy Hart was being sought by the law, his wanted poster showed a string of aliases, making him look, to anyone but another Cherokee, like a hardened criminal. I know a girl called Chicken and a man called Boss or Bossy, and I've heard of one called Monkey.

Other Indians are just as crazy as Cherokees when it comes to names. Among the Crows, Robert Old Horn is called Corky and has the traditional name of He Throws Himself Away, although some call him Garbage Can. Lloyd Old Coyote was called Mickey. And Robert Whitekiller, Cherokee, met and befriended an old Sioux Indian in North Dakota named Roman (emphasis on the second syllable) White Horse. White Horse told Whitekiller that they traded names. Later, Whitekiller went to visit White Horse's grave, but the name on the stone was "Robert Whitekiller." Robert still uses it, however.

Cherokee (and other Indian) names and naming practices can be interesting, they can be funny, they can even be sad. But what should be pointed out, I believe, is that they are not really all that different from the names and naming practices of any other people in the world, even white Englishmen and women. The only real difference is that most white people have forgotten what their names mean and where they came from. But think about it. A Wright is a maker: wheelwright, cartwright, playwright, and so forth. A smith is a worker in something as in Goldsmith, Cold-smith, or just the smith in the smithy. A Bush is most likely something that dogs pee on. Any name has (or had) a meaning at one time, and there was a reason it was bestowed on its owner. When Europeans started passing their surnames along to children, the original meanings were in many cases lost. Even so, they had meanings at one time, even as Cherokee and other Indian names have meanings. The big difference is (to turn around what I said earlier) Indians remember the meaning of theirs.

Will Rogers

Cherokee Writer and So Much More

The following is a speech I gave at the Will Rogers Writers' Workshop in Oklahoma City, Oklahoma, March 17, 2007.

It's a great thrill and a special privilege to be your speaker tonight at the Will Rogers Writers Workshop.[1] I'd like to welcome all of you foreigners to Oklahoma, but since I'm just about the last thing on your schedule, I assume you've already been welcomed. I sure hope so.

It's appropriate in a number of ways to have this workshop, a part of the Oklahoma Centennial Celebration, named after Will Rogers, a Cherokee Indian. Will wasn't the only Indian writer in Oklahoma's early days. There was his friend and fellow Cherokee, John Milton Oskison. There was Lynn Riggs, also Cherokee. And there were a number of other Indian writers who wrote for various newspapers. They were not all Cherokee. There were Creeks, Choctaws, and others. Many of them wrote biting political commentary couched in humor and in dialect. But somehow none of them caught on like Will Rogers. Of course, he was more than just a writer. Will Rogers was a major celebrity.

Will Rogers became famous as an American and as an Oklahoman. Not just as a Cherokee or as an Indian. Indeed, sometimes I think people forget that he was Cherokee or try to make out that it doesn't really matter. But Will was born in 1879 in the Cherokee Nation. Oklahoma did not exist until 1907. His father was a prominent Cherokee Nation politician. Rogers County, Oklahoma, is not named for Will Rogers. It is named for his father, Clem Rogers. Will Rogers was not a citizen of the United States when he was born. He was a Cherokee Nation citizen. U.S. citizenship was put on Cherokees, and other Indians, in what would soon become the new state of Oklahoma, in 1901. That means that Will Rogers was not a U.S. citizen until he was twenty-two years old.

I don't believe that Will ever forgot that he was Cherokee, and I don't believe any of us should ever forget it. Perhaps I'll be shot for bringing this up during the Oklahoma Centennial Celebration, but there is one Will Rogers quotation that is seldom quoted, especially in Oklahoma. Oklahomans would probably prefer that he had never said it, but he did. He said, "We spoiled the best Territory in the World to make a State."

Will's biographer Richard Ketchum said, "Will never possessed the same degree of identification his father had with the Cherokees." I think he was wrong. Often, even when his statements do not mention Indians, they are Indian in character. For example, "You could turn ten college presidents loose in a forest with nothing to eat, or nothing to get it with, and then old so-called 'Ignorant' backwoodsmen, and your presidents wouldn't last a week." Compare this to a statement made by an Indian in a story related by Benjamin Franklin in 1753. A commissioner to the Indians had offered to educate some Indian youth in a college. The Indians responded that "some of their youths had formerly been educated in that college, but it had been observed that for a long time after they returned to their friends, they were absolutely good for nothing being neither acquainted with the true methods of killing deer, catching beaver or surprising an enemy." They made a counteroffer to take some of the English youth and raise them in "the best manner and make men of them."

Most of us have read or heard other comments made by Will Rogers related to his "Cherokeeness" or his "Indianness." Such as, "My ancestors didn't come on the Mayflower, but they met the boat."

He told people he was from Claremore because "nobody but an Indian can pronounce Oologah."

About treaties, he said, "They sent the Indians to Oklahoma. They had a treaty that said, 'You shall have this land as long as grass grows and water flows.' It was not only a good rhyme but looked like a good treaty, and it was till they struck oil. Then the government took it away from us again. They said the treaty refers to water and grass. It didn't say anything about oil."

A historical note on Andrew Jackson, "To tell you the truth I am not so sweet on old Andy. He is the one that run us Cherokees out of Georgia and North Carolina. . . . Old Andy, every time he couldn't find anyone to jump on, would come back and pounce onto us Indians. . . . But old Andy made the White House. . . . The Indians wanted him in there so he could let us alone for a while."

Regarding the Cherokee Nation and the U.S. government, "I was named by an Indian chief, William Penn Adair. He says, Mary, I want another young chief named for me. I name him Will Penn Adair Rogers. I just looked at him when he named me and thought by the time I get big enough to be chief we won't have any more country than a Jay Bird."

He said that he had just enough white blood in him to make his honesty questionable with the Cherokees he went to school with.

Ketchum tells us that Will, around 1899, was known as Rabbit "because of his big ears" and because "he was constantly in motion." He was also always "thinking up devilment." I would venture that Will might have been called Rabbit because he was so much like the old Cherokee Trickster. If you don't know the Cherokee Trickster tales, in which the Trickster is Rabbit, just think of Joel Chandler Harris's Uncle Remus tales with Br'er Rabbit. They are direct borrowings from the Cherokee stories.

Will signed his earliest letters to Betty Blake, who would later become his wife, her "True Friend and Injun Cowboy, W. P. Rogers, Oologah, I.T." I.T. is, of course, Indian Territory.

In one of his letters to Betty, he said that if she did not answer it he would be a "broken-hearted Cherokee cowboy."

When Will went to work for the Texas Jack Wild West Show in South Africa in 1902, he was billed as the Cherokee Kid.

He said, "I was always proud in America to own that I am a Cherokee."

In 1905 at Madison Square Garden in New York City with Zach Mulhall's Wild West Show, an 800-pound steer with a five-foot spread of horns broke loose and ran into the audience. Will roped it and got it under control. One New York paper had a headline that read, "Indian Cowpuncher's Quickness Prevents Harm." An article in another paper read in part, "The Indian Will Rogers . . . headed the steer off."

When Will's first son was born, Clem sent a pair of beaded moccasins for the baby.

According to Betty, Will had "a haphazard way with money that was sometimes frightening." A fairly typical Indian attitude, so I've been told.

In Will's 1922 newspaper column titled "Batting for Lloyd George," Will wrote, "The total share of this goes to the civilization of three young heathens, Rogers by name, and part Cherokee Indians by breeding."

Another historical/political comment: "Why, they didn't discover us till 1492 and the world had had 1492 wars, 1492 peace and economic conferences, all before we was ever heard of."

Here's a good one. "It is certainly gratifying to read about one conference that got somewhere. The Navajo Indians held a conference and decided that they could get along without the services of about twenty-five white officeholders that had been appointed to help look after them. The Indians said that they were doing it to save the white man money. Who said the Indians didn't have any humor?"

When he had trouble obtaining a passport because he did not have a birth certificate, he said, "You see in the early days of the Indian Territory where I was born there was no such thing as birth certificates. You being there was certificate enough. We generally took for granted if you were there you must have at some time been born."

In 1925, writing about the funeral of his sister in Chelsea, Oklahoma, he said, "I am out in Oklahoma, among my People, my Cherokee People, who don't expect a laugh for everything I say."

Ketchum wrote that when Will was home in Oklahoma in the springtime, "there would be tiny wild onions scrambled with eggs." That is a Cherokee dish that my wife likes to prepare to this day, and I love to eat.

After Charles Curtis, who was a Kaw Indian, was nominated for vice president, Will said that "it was the first time we have ever got a break—the only American that has ever run for that high office. Come on, Injun, if you are elected, let's run the white people out of this country."

Ketchum mentions Will's friendship with Admiral Jocko Clark, calling Clark a "former Oklahoman" without mentioning the fact that Clark was also Cherokee.

In 1931, during the Great Depression, Will embarked on a trip through Arkansas, Texas, and Oklahoma, raising money for relief. In eighteen days he raised $225,000, with pledges of more to come. His only requests were that every cent go to the needy, and that a portion of the Oklahoma funds go specifically to help Cherokees.

So much for the question of Will Rogers's Cherokeeness. Some seem to delight in pointing out that he had more white blood than Cherokee. He did. So did John Ross, who was principal chief of the Cherokee Nation for around forty years. Cherokees used to determine who was Cherokee by whether the child was born into a clan, or, put another way, because Cherokee clans are matrilineal, whether or not the child's mother was Cherokee. John Ross's mother was Cherokee. So was Will Rogers's mother.

Will is for us a transitional character, a personality who links the Old West with the so-called modern age. He told a story about his father driving a herd of cattle from Claremore, Indian Territory, now Oklahoma, to Kansas City. Finding no market in Kansas City, he drove them on to St. Louis. And Will was killed in 1935 in an airplane crash.

I don't think any of us can put a finger on exactly what was the secret of Will Rogers's tremendous success and the fact that it has lasted, but I think that part of it was that he could say anything, insult anyone, and get away with it because he said it with a grin, he couched it in humor. He always referred to himself as a humorist.

W. C. Fields once said about some of Will's jokes, "The audience howled at those jokes. If I had delivered them, the audience would have swarmed up over the footlights and murdered me. But Rogers can get away with anything."

A small biography of Will Rogers written by Jerome Beatty while Will was still alive, but actually published in 1935 after his death, begins with these few paragraphs:

> The true story of the rise of Will Rogers, the Cherokee Indian cowhand from Oologah, Indian Territory, is perhaps the most amazing tale that could be written about any living American.
>
> Equipped with only a minor grade-school education, still unable to spell, lacking the ability to turn out a paragraph that would pass the English teachers, he is one of America's highest-paid authors.
>
> Scorning the art of make-up, with only a catch-as-catch-can knowledge of the intricate science of acting as known to Edwin Booth and Richard Mansfield and the Barrymores, he has become probably the most popular actor in this country.
>
> With a voice utterly untrained and a style of delivery that makes the elocutionists writhe in pain, he is a radio star who has received as much $1,000 a minute for a twelve-minute talk.
>
> In his best days as a cowpuncher he made about $25 a month.
>
> His average income for the last three or four years has been more than $1,500 a day.

As fascinating as this little encapsulation is, the part that we should be most interested in here, at this workshop, is the part that says, "Equipped with only a minor grade-school education, still unable to spell, lacking the ability to turn out a paragraph that would pass the English teachers, he is one of America's highest-paid authors."

How did this come about? Beatty says that Will "was with the *Follies* when he became a writer. . . . The *New York Times* asked permission to reprint his comment upon the news of the day. He gave it to them and he suddenly found out that people were interested in what he wrote; that even without his delivery, his lines were funny. So a syndicate was started, and he wrote a hundred words of comment every day." After that, he published a number of books, made up mostly of his newspaper columns. *The Cowboy Philosopher on the Peace Conference* (1919), *The Cowboy Philosopher on Prohibition* (1919), *What We Laugh At* (1920), *Illiterate Digest* (1924), *Letters of a Self-Made Diplomat to His President* (1927), and others.

We often tell writing students or would-be writers to take courses in creative writing. Will never took such courses. He never even finished school. We tell them to read, read, read. Will himself said that he seldom read a book. He was too busy roping calves. He did read newspapers—voraciously. He did not do anything to prepare himself for a writing career. In fact, he never pursued a writing career. It came after him. Granted, it was a small part of his career. He was a performing artist, an actor, a highly sought after speaker, a radio personality, and a writer. But the main word in that list is, I think, personality.

As Beatty wrote:

> What is it that has made Will Rogers? The West could produce a hundred cowhands, when he was a Wild West show performer, who could rope a steer and ride a horse as well as he. There are hundreds of men in Hollywood and on Broadway, New York City, who can act rings around him. Newspaper and magazine offices are filled with people who can write better English than Will Rogers. Any radio announcer knows more than Will Rogers does about the technique of delivery over the microphone.
>
> But they haven't Will Rogers' brain, his wit, his common sense or his personality.
>
> They haven't Will Rogers' ability to remain just himself, a friend of everybody who deserves a friend.
>
> . . . Will Rogers, who started from nothing and who reached the top, is still the crude, kindly, witty, friendly fellow who used to lean against a hitching post in an Oklahoma cow town—a cheerful cuss, always making fun of people in a whimsical way that makes everybody laugh, even the folks he is making fun of.

Well, that's one way of looking at it. I don't suppose that any of us can ever come up with a really satisfactory answer to the question, "What is it that has made Will Rogers?" Let's just be thankful that the world had him for the time it did, and that he left enough behind for those of us who came along too late to enjoy him in his lifetime to still read, watch, listen to, and feel as if we do know him.

Linking Back

Linking back. Joseph Campbell said in a television interview once that the word "religion" means "linking back." That's what I do constantly in this Cherokee country, now called northeast Oklahoma, of which Tahlequah is the center—*Ayehli*.

Linking back. I live in Tahlequah, the capital city of the Cherokee Nation. Not even paved roads (often in need of repair), new buildings, and automobile traffic can interfere with the linking back process. I can drive down Muskogee Avenue, the main street in Tahlequah, past the bars and the banks, stopping at the traffic lights, smelling the exhaust fumes from the heavy traffic, reading the sometimes gaudy signs of new businesses, pizza parlors, fast-food restaurants, car lots, liquor stores, auto-parts stores, the new Wal-Mart Super Center—and not even these distractions can drive from my mind the constant realization that I am on a street where Principal Chief John Ross rode in his carriage, where General Stand Watie led his Cherokee Confederate troops, where hundreds of Indians thronged when the Cherokee Nation hosted the great intertribal Indian Council in 1843.

Linking back. That, I think, is the secret of the Indians' attachment to the land, really of any human being's concern with place. We have reverence for a particular place because of our knowledge of or sense of what was there before, and our connection with the past gives us a reason for being, a sense of belonging, and a feeling for, if not real knowledge of, our origins. It defines us. It tells us who we are. Madness is, I think, a broken link. The chain that links us back holds the anchor for our sanity.

I live in the Cherokee Nation. I do not consider that I live in Oklahoma. Of course, I have to deal with the reality of Oklahoma. It came in on top of the Cherokee Nation and imposed its own laws, and I have accepted that reality. I have accepted it, and I live with it, because I want to live in Tahlequah, in the Cherokee Nation.

One of the many things that I love about living in Tahlequah is that I am constantly surrounded by reminders of the history that I am so much involved with. When I drive to town to check my mail, I go along Water Street, the first road leading from the capitol, where Chief John Ross and others went to work, to Park Hill, where Ross and some of the others had their homes. I think about Ross in his buggy, making his way to the government offices on the square. If I drive all the way downtown, I will see the old capitol building, rebuilt after a fire in 1873. Ned Christie and other council members about whom I have read and written were in that building, and I thrill when I think that the Cherokee Nation, having lost all of its government buildings at Oklahoma statehood in 1907, owns the building once again.

From the south side of the capitol square, I can look across the street at the old Cherokee National Supreme Court building, the first two-story brick structure built in what is now the state of Oklahoma. I can go one block farther south and see the old Cherokee National Prison. All of these historic buildings are once again Cherokee Nation property. A few blocks north, on Muskogee Avenue, the last of the old buildings still stands. What Northeastern State University now calls Seminary Hall is the old Cherokee National Female Seminary. It's not the original female seminary, which was located south of town on land now occupied by the Cherokee Heritage Center. When the original burned in 1887, it was rebuilt north of town. My grandmother went to school there.

In 1890, when my grandmother was born, there was no state of Oklahoma. She was born a citizen of the Cherokee Nation. When Oklahoma became a state in 1907, she became, by U.S. law, a citizen of the new state of Oklahoma. The Cherokee Nation was effectively dismantled. Its capitol building was taken over by the new Cherokee County and used as a county courthouse. Its National Prison was taken over by the county for a county jail. Its Cherokee National Female Seminary was taken by the state and became a state normal school that has since developed into Northeastern

State University. Its newspaper, the *Cherokee Phoenix*, was purchased for a song by someone in Fort Gibson.

My father was born in 1920, deprived of citizenship in an independent Cherokee Nation by a short nineteen years, and I myself was born only thirty-three years after the onset of Oklahoma statehood. I feel that loss keenly and every day. That is another result of living in Tahlequah: living with the history on a daily basis, being constantly aware of the things that have taken place over the years, realizing daily that the past is not that long ago, that in fact it is still with us and will always be with us.

The United States of America signed thirty-three treaties with the Cherokee Nation. In each of them, it took land away from the Cherokees, and in each, it promised that it would not come back for more. In each, it pledged perpetual peace and friendship. In some, it forbade American citizens to trespass and squat on Cherokee lands and said that if any did so, the Cherokee Nation could deal with them as it pleased. Yet white Americans did move onto Cherokee land, and the government did nothing about it. When the Cherokees attempted to do something about it, the U.S. government—to protect its citizens and the interests of its citizens, and following the conflict thus generated—would sign a new treaty with the Cherokees, and more land would be wrenched away from the Cherokees. It is a pattern almost as old as contact between the Cherokees and the English colonists.

When I first visited the old Cherokee country in South Carolina, I was awestruck by its beauty, but I was also saddened and angered at the theft of all that from my ancestors. My feelings were intensified when I found the name of one of my own ancestors on local maps. I made a second trip to the old Cherokee country, this time to North Carolina, where I met for the first time many Eastern Cherokees, descendants of those hardy few who managed to avoid the disastrous Cherokee Removal of 1838–39 known as the Trail of Tears. They welcomed me home. One gracious woman said, "My father always told us, 'When anyone from Oklahoma comes out here, welcome them into your home. They're your relatives.'" I knew that those people were living where we all should live, and I realized that more fully when my friend Tom Belt took me to visit the site of the ancient town of Keetoowah, the mother town, the town from which all the other Cherokee towns developed, the town where we all come from. It was perhaps the most profound experience of my life.

Why? Perhaps it was linking back. Linking back, if not to the actual very beginning of time, at least to as far back as I need to go. To the beginnings of my Cherokee People as we know them today. The ancient mound that stood in the center of the town is not as high as it was in the beginning, but it is still there, still visible. It was the center of all ceremonial activity of the early Cherokees, and it is being used in that way once again. There are men buried around the perimeter of the mound. They are most probably the priests of that ancient time. Standing around the mound today, I can feel—something. A deep and profound feeling of awe and respect and admiration and, yes, a sense of loss. But the sense of loss is minimized standing there in Keetoowah, and the primary sensation in my breast is that magnificent feeling of "linking back."

The Freedmen Controversy

The April 2007 issue of the *Cherokee Phoenix*, in a front-page story titled "Voters Amend Cherokee Constitution," said the following: "Cherokee citizens on March 3 voted at a ratio of nearly 3-to-1 to amend the Cherokee Nation Constitution restricting tribal citizenship to descendants of Indians listed by blood on the Dawes Rolls and excluding descendants of Freedmen and adopted whites." Quoted in the same article, Cherokee Nation Principal Chief Chad Smith said, "The Cherokee people exercised the most basic democratic right, the right to vote. . . . Their voice is clear as to who should be citizens of the Cherokee Nation. No one else has the right to make that determination."

On the surface, it all makes good sense. The citizenship of the Cherokee Nation should be made up of Cherokee people, that is, of people of Cherokee blood. It could easily be argued that it should also be made up of people of Cherokee blood who are part of Cherokee communities, or of people who have at least one-quarter degree of Cherokee blood, or of people who speak the Cherokee language, or . . . This argument could go on and on. But that is not the issue here. The issue here is the Cherokee Freedman Roll, how it came about, and whether it can simply be discarded. Two important and little-known books have been written on the history of this subject. The first is *Red over Black: Black Slavery among the Cherokee Indians* by R. Halliburton, Jr., published in 1977, and the second is *The Cherokee Freedman: From Emancipation to American Citizenship* by Daniel F. Littlefield, Jr., published in 1978.[1] Taken together, these two books provide a thorough history of black slavery and its aftermath among the Cherokees. Much of what follows about the historical background of this controversial subject has been gleaned from these two books.

Black slavery was almost certainly introduced among the Cherokees in the 1600s by English traders. Many of the traders lived with the Cherokees, and some built themselves large plantations. They married Cherokee women and started mixed-blood Cherokee families, and they bought black slaves to work their plantations. Other traders brought black slaves into the Cherokee Nation to sell to Cherokees. There also developed a brisk business in stealing and selling black slaves. It should be mentioned here that Cherokees often became slaves themselves. "In 1693 a tribal delegation lodged an official protest to the Royal Governor of South Carolina. They charged that the Congaree, Esau (Catawba), and Savannah Indians were capturing Cherokees and selling them into slavery."[2]

In 1730, the seven Cherokees who visited England with Sir Alexander Cuming signed a treaty with the king at Whitehall in which they agreed to capture any runaway slaves and return them to their English masters or to the governor. The British government encouraged slavery among the Cherokees, occasionally even giving slaves to important Cherokees as gifts, while the colonists did their best to discourage it by enacting laws against whites taking black slaves into the Cherokee Nation and against whites who lived among the Cherokees owning slaves. The colonists' stance was partly a result of fear that Cherokees would steal their slaves.

The first Cherokee known by name to be a slave owner was Nancy Ward, who, in 1755, following the Battle of Taliwa with the Creeks, received a black slave as part of the spoils of war. She bought other slaves after that. But as time went on, "Most of the well-known and influential Cherokees were becoming slave owners. Such influential Cherokees as Ross, Vann, Foreman, Alberty, Scales, Boudinot, Lowrey, Rogers, McNair, Ridge, Chisholm, Downing, Drew, Martin, Nave, Jolly, Hildebrand, Webber, and Adair became slaveholders."[3]

During the long off-and-on wars with, first, the English colonies and then with the new United States, the Cherokees slowly moved out of their towns and began living on individual farms, many of which became plantations. Many Cherokees, therefore, like their white contemporaries in the South, became cotton growers and, of course, slave owners. This form of black slavery was learned from the whites, and it was partly, if not largely, responsible for the Cherokees and their four neighboring tribes of Creeks, Choctaws, Chickasaws, and Seminoles becoming known as the Five Civilized Tribes.

Major Ridge, a full-blood, was the first Cherokee plantation owner "of magnitude," according to Halliburton. He ran a huge plantation known as "Chieftains," with a two-story log house with glass windows, two kitchens outside the back door, a smokehouse, two stables, a lumber house, and cabins for the thirty black slaves. Ridge had three hundred acres planted with corn, cotton, tobacco, wheat, oats, indigo, sweet potatoes, and Irish potatoes. In addition, he had orchards of peach, apple, cherry, plum, and quince trees; a vineyard; a nursery; and a garden. He had hogs and cattle in his pastures.

By 1811, according to the *Christian Observer*, published in London, there were 583 slaves in the Cherokee Nation, which had a total Cherokee population of 12,395. The status of blacks, slave or otherwise, among the Cherokees is clear from the case of Shoe Boot in 1824. When Shoe Boot's wife left him, he married his slave, Lucy. She bore him two children. By law they were also his slaves. He petitioned the Cherokee National Council for free status for his children. His request was granted, but he was warned by the council that such marriages were not socially acceptable. Almost immediately afterward, the council passed a law prohibiting intermarriage with blacks. It imposed a fine of $50 on offenders, and further fifty-nine stripes on the bare back for any Indian or white male offender and twenty-nine stripes on the bare back for any Indian or white female offender. Halliburton says that "the Cherokees were adamant in their determination not to become racially identified with a subject people whom they regarded—as did their white neighbors—as their servants and inferiors."[4] In 1824, the *Cherokee Phoenix* reported that there were 1,038 black slaves in the Cherokee Nation.

When whites began agitating for removal of the Cherokees from their ancient homelands in the old South, some Cherokees began moving west. By 1811, they were settled in Arkansas. They had with them their slaves, so there were Cherokee slave owners in Arkansas and Cherokee slave owners still in the old country in the East. By 1835, a census in the old Cherokee Nation showed 1,592 slaves. The Western Cherokees, those in Arkansas, had taken their slaves with them when they first moved west. The numbers of slaves are not known, but there were plenty, judging from the laws enacted by the Western Cherokees and by conflicts they had with their white neighbors over stealing slaves. We do know that in 1829 and 1832, over two hundred more slaves were brought into the area by immigrating Cherokees.

In 1838 and 1839, those Cherokees who endured the infamous Trail of Tears brought their slaves with them, too. Halliburton indicates that between 125 and 175 blacks were among the 4,000 or so who died along the way. In the new Cherokee Nation, established in the West following the Trail of Tears in what is now northeastern Oklahoma, a new Cherokee constitution was written and adopted in 1839. Blacks were no better off than before.

> Article III, Section 5. No person shall be eligible to a seat in the National Council but a free Cherokee male citizen who shall have attained to the age of twenty-five years.
>
> The descendants of Cherokee men by all free women except the African race . . . shall be entitled to all the rights and privileges of this Nation . . . as well as the posterity of Cherokee women by all free men. No person who is of negro or mulatto parentage, either by the father or mother's side, shall be eligible to hold any office of profit, honor, or trust under this Government.

By the 1850s, slavery had become a heated issue, not only in the United States but also in the Cherokee Nation. An 1859 census declared that there were 21,000 Cherokees and noncitizens living in the Cherokee Nation and 9,000 blacks, mostly slaves. Rachel Carolyn Eaton, in *John Ross and the Cherokee Indians*, says that there were 4,000 or more slaves.[5] The Blue Lodge (later known as the Knights of the Golden Circle and the Southern Rights Party) was formed by mostly mixed-blood slave owners, and the Pin Indians were organized, partly as an abolitionist group.

When the Civil War broke out, Principal Chief John Ross attempted to keep the Cherokee Nation out of it, but in spite of all his efforts, the Nation was dragged into it. Stand Watie raised a regiment of Cherokee troops for the Confederacy, and in August 1861 even Ross gave in. Because the Union abandoned the Cherokee Nation and because he feared that the Confederates would overrun the Nation, Ross signed a treaty with the Confederacy. Less than a year later, from the safety of Philadelphia, Ross repudiated the Confederate treaty.

As the Civil War raged in the Cherokee Nation, Cherokee families, many with their slaves, fled the Cherokee Nation, some going south to Texas, some moving into the Choctaw Nation, some to Kansas, and some to other places. Federal Cherokees met in 1863 and passed an emancipation act. However, at the end of the Civil War, the United States apparently (conveniently) forgot everything except General Stand Watie's "Confederate" Cherokees and Chief Ross's less-than-one-year treaty with the Confederacy. In 1866, the United States forced a reconstruction treaty on the Cherokee Nation.

The United States said that all existing treaties with the Cherokee Nation were void because of the Cherokees' involvement with the Confederacy. The new 1866 treaty was devastating to the Cherokee Nation, but for the purposes of this essay, only those portions that dealt with the former Cherokee slaves will be looked at.

In Article 9, the treaty recognized that the Cherokee Nation had "voluntarily, in February, eighteen hundred and sixty-three, by act of the national council, forever abolished slavery," and it further said that "all freedmen who have been liberated by voluntary act of their former owners or by law, as well as all free colored persons who were in the country at the commencement of the rebellion, and are nonresidents therein, or who may return within six months, and their descendants, shall have all the rights of native Cherokees."

Following up the signing of the Treaty of 1866, the Cherokee Nation, on November 28, 1866, amended Article 3 of its constitution at a convention of Cherokee people in Tahlequah. Section 5 of Article 2 was amended to read as follows:

> All native born Cherokees, all Indians, and whites legally members of the Nation by adoption, and all freedmen who have been liberated by voluntary act of their former owners or by law, as well as free colored persons who were in the country at the commencement of the rebellion, and are now residents therein, or who may return within six months from the 19th day of July, 1866, and their descendants, who reside within the limits of the Cherokee Nation, shall be taken, and deemed to be, citizens of the Cherokee Nation.

Many of the freedmen who had left (or been taken out of) the Cherokee Nation during the war did not know of the six months stipulation and did not, therefore, return in time to take advantage of the situation. Many of those who did know lacked the means to travel. Some Cherokee freedmen did return, however, and some took up residence and put in crops. Some Cherokees wanted them removed from the Cherokee Nation as noncitizens. Littlefield says that for forty years following the Treaty of 1866, "freedmen rights were a constant source of conflict between the Cherokees and U.S. officials."[6] By 1869, he says, the Cherokee Nation had large numbers of intruders moving in. Some of them were blacks who claimed to be freedmen with legitimate claims to Cherokee citizenship. By 1870, many of the freedmen had become productive members of Cherokee society, while many Cherokees viewed them as a problem that had been thrust upon them by the federal government.

The real sore point, however, was the freedmen who had returned to the Cherokee Nation after the Civil War, but had returned too late, either not knowing about the six-month stipulation or not being able to get back in time. The Cherokee Nation insisted upon a strict interpretation of the treaty on that matter, but the Cherokee agent, William Davis, was reluctant to remove them because removal would mean, in many cases, separating families. Some U.S. officials insisted that the Cherokee Nation was obligated to take in the freedmen whether or not they had returned within the time limit.

Littlefield says that "most of the freedmen were farmers. . . . Some freedmen owned businesses such as barber shops, blacksmith shops, general stores, and restaurants. Others worked for the Cherokees as ferry operators, printers' devils, and cotton gin operators. Still others were teachers, and at least two were postmasters."[7] Some could not speak English, speaking only the Cherokee language.

The Cherokee Nation practiced segregation, establishing some schools for the children of freedmen, but not allowing those children to attend schools for the Cherokees. The freedmen were also not allowed admittance in the Cherokee Nation's orphan asylum. They were denied access to the Cherokee male and female seminaries. When freedmen complained to the chief, William Potter Ross, he claimed that there was no prejudice in the Cherokee Nation.

Freedmen were allowed to vote, however, and they were courted by candidates for office from both political parties. One freedman was elected to the Cherokee National Council in 1875. He served one term. There were some voices of reason among the Cherokees. The editor of the *Cherokee Advocate*, in 1877, wrote, "As one people we have no use for different classes. Let the maxim be honor to whom honor is due, and not to 'class, color, or condition.'" But blacks outside the Cherokee Nation viewed the Cherokee Nation as a haven, and many from the old South went to the Cherokee Nation seeking better opportunities. Yet there was racism in the Cherokee Nation. In 1894, the editor of the *Cherokee Advocate* wrote, "Be men and fight off the barnacles that now infest our country in the shape of non-citizens, free Arkansas niggers and traitors."

Rolls were taken of the freedmen, and each was challenged by the Cherokee Nation as defective. Lawyers were hired by both sides, and vast amounts of money changed hands, most going to the lawyers. Accusations of fraud were thrown at both sides. Attempts were made to remove those freedmen who were identified as intruders. Chief Lewis Downing attempted to aid the freedman, but the council thwarted his efforts. Chief William Potter Ross, who succeeded Downing, attempted to get the council to recognize not only the freedmen whose claims to citizenship were not disputed but also to bring into the fold those who had returned to the Cherokee Nation too late. He, too, was unsuccessful.

Then there were the freedmen whose citizenship was not disputed but who were refused a share in per capita payments paid to Cherokee citizens. There are several such documented cases. Commissions were appointed, made their reports, and were dissolved. New commissions were appointed. Freedmen were lied to by government officials. Some freedmen swore out affidavits to commissions and failed to appear before the commission because one of the commissioners wrote them a letter in which he said that "the department had never recognized the authority of the Cherokees to decide who were and were not citizens of the Nation and until such recognition was given, it was not necessary for the freedmen to attend meetings of the court of commissioners." When they failed to appear, their cases were rejected.

Chief Dennis Wolfe Bushyhead tried to help the freedman in their cause but like Chief Downing and Chief Ross before him, was defeated by the council. The 1880 census showed 1,976 freedmen recognized by the Cherokee Nation as citizens and 1,821 whom the Cherokee Nation considered intruders. Into all of this confused mess the idea of Oklahoma statehood intruded. The Curtis Act, passed in 1892, forced allotment on the Cherokee Nation and called for an end to the Cherokee Nation government. The Dawes Commission was charged with preparing a final Cherokee roll, including a freedman roll. Although the Curtis Act called for dissolution of the Cherokee Nation government, future acts of Congress extended the life of the government, the last one "under limited conditions until tribal affairs were closed." When the Dawes Roll was finally closed, 41,835 citizens were enrolled. Of these, 4,919 were freedmen.

Just about everyone believed that the Cherokee Nation was no more. The efforts of the freedmen to achieve citizenship in the Cherokee Nation stopped. As recently as 1976, a Cherokee was heard to say, when asked if he had gone to the Cherokee Nation offices in Tahlequah for help with a problem, "I went into Tahlequah to that Indian office." He had no idea that the Cherokee Nation had been reconstituted. Such knowledge was slow in coming. The Cherokee Nation had been effectively put to sleep in 1907 with Oklahoma statehood. It was aroused again in 1973 with new elections. During the time between those two dates, the president of the United States had appointed the Cherokee chiefs. They came to be known as "chiefs for a day." No one took them too seriously.

Once the Cherokee Nation began functioning again, it took a few years for the freedman controversy to resurface. But it did. Largely through the efforts of Marilyn Vann, president of the Descendants of Freedmen of the Five Civilized Tribes, the freedmen descendants of the Cherokees and other freedmen began pressing their case once again. Following much debate, the Cherokee Nation called for a vote of Cherokee citizens to determine who could be a Cherokee citizen. The result of that vote, held on March 3, 2007, was to restrict tribal citizenship to descendants of Indians listed by blood on the Dawes Roll. Thus any black who has Cherokee blood and whose ancestor was listed on the Dawes Roll can be a citizen, but any black descended from any former Cherokee slave listed on the Dawes Roll as a freedman cannot.

The vote is being hailed by some, including the current chief of the Cherokee Nation, as a powerful blow for tribal sovereignty. The Cherokee people have determined who should be Cherokee citizens, he says. "No one else has the right to make that determination." He said the vote exercised the tribe's sovereignty and self-governance. "It was a right of self-government, affirmed in twenty-three treaties with Great Britain and the United States and paid dearly with 4,000 lives on the Trail of Tears," he said.

Even the highly respected American Indian scholar Clara Sue Kidwell, director of the Native American Studies Program at the

University of Oklahoma, backed up Chief Smith's statements, saying, "What the Cherokee Nation is doing is an exercise of one of the very basic forms of self-government. It's a tribe's sovereign right to determine its own membership; even the United States does it."[8]

There is no arguing that it is the right of any sovereignty to determine its own membership or citizenry. And it is right and proper for Indian tribes to assert their sovereignty and their sovereign rights. When Kidwell says that "the very act of signing treaties . . . is a recognition of sovereignty," she is absolutely correct. Federal Indian law and policy recognize that Indian tribes were originally sovereignties, and they still are, but with certain qualifications: First, if they have given up any rights of sovereignty in any treaties they have signed with the United States. Second, if any federal law has taken away any of their rights of sovereignty.

The Cherokee Nation, like every other Indian tribe in the United States, is therefore a limited sovereignty. And even though signing a treaty is an act of sovereignty, by exercising that act, the Cherokee Nation also limits its sovereignty. In the case of the Treaty of 1866, the treaty limited the Cherokee Nation's sovereignty by giving the United States the right to include the Cherokee freedmen "as well as all free colored persons who were in the country at the commencement of the rebellion . . . all the rights of native Cherokees." The words "citizen" and "citizenship" are not used; however, the implication is clear, and if it is not clear to anyone, such as the current principal chief or the current chair of Native American studies at the University of Oklahoma, the Cherokee Council made it clear on November 28, 1866, with the amendment to Article 3, Section 5, of the Cherokee Constitution, which, once again, reads:

> All native born Cherokees, all Indians, and whites legally members of the Nation by adoption, and all freedmen who have been liberated by voluntary act of their former owners or by law, as well as free colored persons who were in the country at the commencement of the rebellion, and are now residents therein, or who may return within six months from the 19th day of July, 1866, and their descendants, who

reside within the limits of the Cherokee Nation, shall be taken, and deemed to be, citizens of the Cherokee Nation.

What could be more clear? Of course, a constitution can be amended, and that is what happened on March 3, 2007. But a treaty cannot be broken, not without consequences. Indian tribes all over the United States have been asserting their treaty rights in recent years. What kind of a precedent is the Cherokee Nation setting by breaking a treaty? Does that give the United States the right to break that same treaty? Does it give it the right to break other treaties? Or only treaties with the Cherokee Nation or treaties with any Indian tribe? With all Indian tribes?

Opponents of the rights of tribal sovereignty have for years been calling for the abrogation of all Indian treaties, claiming that they are old and out of date and no longer applicable. Will the action of the Cherokee Nation regarding the 1866 treaty give those opponents further ammunition? I should think that it will.

I have one further thought about this recent Cherokee Nation action and the reasons given for it. If the Cherokee Nation is really serious about exercising its sovereignty and determining its own membership, then why the hell does it continue to use the Dawes Commission Roll, which was put together by the U.S. government and then closed by the U.S. government? The Cherokee Nation does not have a current roll. It is not allowed to have one by the U.S. Congress. The Dawes Roll is the only roll, and when the last original enrollee on the Dawes Roll dies, there will be no Cherokee Nation roll. When the Cherokee Nation lists anyone as a current tribal member, it puts him or her on a "tribal membership list." It "registers" him or her only.

I have never read anything about the Dawes Roll that did not condemn the roll for being inefficient, faulty, even fraudulent, or talked to anyone about the Dawes Roll who did not agree with that assessment. Legitimate Cherokee citizens of mixed blood who could get away with it were enrolled as less Cherokee than they really were in order to be able to sell or lease their land sooner. Some whites without a legitimate claim were falsely enrolled. Many traditional full-bloods actually avoided enrollment and have descendants today who cannot get registered with the Cherokee Nation because of that. Chief Smith's own great-grandfather, the great Redbird Smith, refused to enroll until he was thrown into jail in Muskogee and told he would be kept there until he enrolled. At that point, he caved in.

The recent Cherokee Nation election challenged a portion of the Dawes Roll, that portion labeled "freedmen." Why in the world did it not challenge the whole damned thing?

We have not yet heard the end of this controversy. According to the *Tahlequah Daily Press* of March 18, 2007,

> U.S. District Judge Henry Kennedy did leave open the possibility the Freedman case would be back in court if their citizenship rights were removed.
>
> "He did say if they were voted out we would be back in court," Jon Velie, an attorney for the Freedmen, said.

And Marilyn Vann says the freedmen will continue to fight the election in federal court.

There are indeed three lawsuits in federal court at this writing. In the meantime, Representative Diane Watson, Democrat from California, has introduced a bill in Congress to cut off federal funding to the Cherokee Nation (approximately $300 million a year) until such time as the Cherokee Nation restores the freedmen descendants to full tribal citizenship, because the Cherokee Nation has violated a treaty. In response, Principal Chief Chad Smith said that we should let the courts decide. The Cherokee Nation claims, in fact, that the freedmen are enjoying that status right now while waiting for the court decisions.

There is no doubt that there will be many more developments to this issue by the time this book sees print. Who knows? When you read this essay, the whole issue may have been resolved. That may be too much to hope for though. After all, it has been with us now for 141 years.

John Oskison and Me

My first novel, *Back to Malachi*, was published in 1986 by Doubleday. It was actually written way back in 1968 or 1969, but it took me all that time to find a publisher for it. I always thought that it was because I did not know what I was doing. In fact, I have said that it took me all those years to discover just what it is an agent does for a writer and then to figure out how to do those things for myself. None of that is true, except for the dates. When the book was finally published, I went looking for a paperback house to reprint it. I got a copy of it into the hands of the then editor of western books at Pocketbooks. Later, he said to me, "I like it, but I couldn't possibly publish a western with an Indian as a main character." I'm a slow learner, but perhaps that was also the reason it took so long for that book to get into print.

I had written *Back to Malachi* out of anger and frustration. I was fresh out of graduate school and working at my first teaching job as an instructor of English at Northern Illinois University (NIU) in DeKalb. I did not like the school, and I did not like DeKalb. I did not like Illinois. I have been an Oklahoman since birth. It was too far north, and it was too cold. DeKalb was an agricultural community. The population was mostly farmers or at least farmer-types. There were canneries as well, and they usually permeated the air with an awful stench. The campus population called the town population hicks, and the townspeople said that the faculty of the university were a bunch of commies.

I don't believe the faculty was a bunch of commies (although I knew one who claimed to be), but they were a bunch of snobs. The old town-gown jokes and all of the rank-consciousness tales I had heard were all too real at NIU. I was so uncomfortable and so unhappy there that I began thinking about home almost constantly. But thinking about home, I thought about the past. I became obsessed with the Indian Territory days, those days between the end of the Civil War and Oklahoma statehood. My grandfather had been a young man just before Oklahoma statehood, and remembered Indian Territory well. He often told tales of those days. So I remembered his tales, and I began reading anything I could find about Indian Territory, especially about the Cherokee Nation.

In the process of all this reading, I came across several stories about Ned Christie. They all said that he was a full-blood Cherokee who could speak both Cherokee and English. He was a blacksmith and a gunsmith, and he had been elected to the Cherokee National Council. But, they said, like all Indians, he could not handle his liquor, and one day when he was intoxicated in Tahlequah, he had killed a deputy U.S. marshal named Dan Maples. He then went "on the scout." Then he commenced to commit numerous robberies, murders, and rapes, until, after four and a half years of pursuit, a posse of deputy marshals finally cornered him and killed him.

At first I did not question these stories, but then I realized that it was strange that a man who was called the worst outlaw ever to infest the Indian Territory was not accused of a single crime other than the killing of Dan Maples. I knew that the details of many of the crimes committed by the James Gang, the Daltons, Bill Doolin, and others were well known and widely published. Why then, I asked myself, could I not find one crime committed by the worst outlaw detailed?

After quite a lot of frustrating research, I sat down one day and found myself writing a novel. It was not about Ned Christie, although one major scene in the novel was borrowed quite obviously from the Ned Christie story. Rather, it was a novel in which I attempted to show how and why a Cherokee in those days might have been called an outlaw and pursued as such.

I wrote two more novels for Doubleday, both with Cherokee main characters, and both were published, but I still could not get a paperback publisher for either of them. Then I wrote three western novels with no Indian characters for the M. Evans Company, and Pocketbooks brought them all out in paperback. Next I wrote three original paperback westerns for Pocketbooks. I got a call from my agent. She said that the new Pocketbooks western books editor would like to talk to me. I called him. He said that their editorial policy regarding Indian main characters had not changed, but, he said, "Why don't you write me a book with an Indian and a white guy as buddies? Buddy novels are big right now. I think I can get away with that." I told him, "I think that's been done already. They called it the Lone Ranger and Tonto, but I'll see what I can do."

So I wrote him a novel called *Strange Company*, in which I had an ignorant farm boy from Iowa named Benjamin Franklin Lacey, who thinks that he was named after a president of the United States, get thrown together with a college-educated Cherokee named Roderick Dhu Walker. Pocketbooks bought it, and I wrote two more with the same characters. Then I had another call from the editor. This time he said, "What you're doing is all right, but why don't you just go ahead and write what you want to write?"

Go-Ahead Rider was published in paperback in 1990 by Pocketbooks. It had taken me four years, but I had completely overturned Pocketbooks' policy regarding Indians in western novels. What I did not realize was that it had taken much longer than that. I was not the first. No. John Milton Oskison had entered the fray long before me.

Oskison was born in 1874 in Vinita, the Cherokee Nation, in what is now northeastern Oklahoma. He went to Willie Halsell College there, as did Will Rogers, and the two became lifelong friends. Oskison went on to Stanford, the first American Indian student there, and finished his BA in 1898. While at Stanford, he wrote for its magazine, *Sequoia*. Following his graduation, he enrolled at Harvard to study literature. He wrote a short story, "Only the Master Shall Praise," which won the *Century* magazine competition for college graduates and brought him national attention.

He continued to write short stories for a time, publishing such tales as "The Problem of Old Harjo," "The Fall of King Chris," and "When the Grass Grew Long" in magazines such as *Century*, *North American Review*, and *McClure's*. From 1903 until 1912, Oskison edited a daily newspaper, and he became financial editor for

Collier's magazine. He also did some writing for the *Saturday Evening Post* and wrote articles on finance that were syndicated in a number of publications. As his reputation grew, he was sought after for his opinion on Indian affairs.

Oskison has been faulted for his ideas on Indian affairs in more recent years. He was an assimilationist, believing that Indians had to learn to live in the white people's world. But those ideas need to be looked at in the context of their times. By the time of Oskison's birth, the movement toward Oklahoma statehood was already under way. The Cherokee Nation was effectively dismantled in 1898 by the Curtis Act. By the time Oskison was writing about Indian affairs, the Dawes Commission was busy with its nefarious work of enrolling Cherokees in preparation for statehood. W. C. Rogers, principal chief of the Cherokee Nation, was impeached and removed from office in 1905 by the Cherokee National Council and replaced by Frank Boudinot, but the president of the United States refused to recognize the council's action and kept Rogers as chief. Thereafter, the chiefs of the Cherokee Nation were appointed by the president. For the rest of Oskison's life, the Cherokee Nation functioned under the so-called chiefs for a day. Very often they were appointed just for a day, just long enough to get a signature.

The Cherokee allotments, like those of the other of the so-called Five Civilized Tribes, were being stolen regularly and often ruthlessly by the grafters in the new state of Oklahoma. This process has been graphically detailed by Angie Debo in her monumental work, *And Still the Waters Run*, a book that should be required reading by all students in the state of Oklahoma. Cherokees needed to get wise to the ways of white people in order to defend themselves. It would have been difficult for any thinking man of Oskison's time to have ideas other than those Oskison held. On top of everything else, it was still widely if not universally believed that Indians were a vanishing race, that they would all disappear sometime in the not so distant future.

And Oskison's views on current Indian affairs were far different from his views of Indian history. If his short stories and his novels fail to state those views overtly, his biography of Tecumseh does not. In *Tecumseh and His Times* (1938), Oskison pulls no punches.

He is fully and firmly on the side of the Indians. There is no doubt as to where he stands. I suggest, therefore, that he became an assimilationist because he could see no other way.

At any rate, Oskison's career was interrupted by World War I. He served with the American Expeditionary Force in Europe. When he returned to the United States at the end of the war, he turned to writing novels, and as with his short stories, he wrote about the Indian Territory days. In *Wild Harvest* and *Black Jack Davy*, the heroes are white. In 1929, he published *A Texas Titan*, the story of Sam Houston. *Brothers Three* has mixed-blood main characters, and he published his biography of Tecumseh in 1938. He left behind an unpublished novel, *The Singing Bird*, which has recently been published by the University of Oklahoma Press. When he died he was working on his autobiography.

Black Jack Davy has a character in a subplot who seems to have been suggested by Ned Christie. He is called Ned Warrior, and when I first read the novel, I felt that Oskison really wanted to write about Ned Warrior. Sam Houston, of course, had a connection to Cherokees, and I feel as sure as I felt about Ned Warrior that Oskison chose to write about Houston because of his Cherokee connection. The brothers in *Brothers Three* are Cherokees, although they are mixed-bloods and hardly distinguishable from whites. Oskison wanted to write about Cherokees, but the closest he could come to it, because of the demand of his publishers, I am sure, was to write about the white people in the Cherokee Nation, to put Cherokees in the background, and to write about mixed-bloods who were more white than Indian. Had I read these books before I started writing, I would have known what I was going to be up against.

Oskison did write about Tecumseh, and he did so brilliantly. He got away with it, I'm sure, because of Tecumseh's fame and because he was writing history. Then he wrote his most "Indian" novel, *The Singing Bird*. Even in that one, he was careful to write from the point of view of the white missionaries. The white missionaries, however, learn much from the Cherokees around them, so there is much of Cherokee culture, language, and lore in the tale. He never did publish the novel.

When I finally read *The Singing Bird*, I was amazed to discover that Oskison had used some of the same source material for his novel that I had used in my 1995 novel, *Captain Dutch*. The source material is *Reminiscences of the Indians* by the Reverend Cephas Washburn, originally published in 1869. Washburn was the founder and for many years the superintendent of Dwight Mission among the Cherokees. When Washburn arrived in the Cherokee country in Arkansas in 1820, he stopped at the home of a Cherokee man and asked directions to the home of the chief. The Cherokee sent Washburn on a wild goose chase that nearly resulted in Washburn's death. I used that episode in my novel, and Oskison had used it in his. That knowledge brought me even closer in my own mind to Oskison.

I think you may be able to understand at this point why, when I first discovered Oskison and first read his work and as I continued reading him over the years, I identified with him so intently. He was a Cherokee writer who wanted to write about Cherokees. He had done so in his short stories, but when it came to getting novels published, he ran into problems with his publishers. He wrote around what he really wanted to write about. I imagine that he was very much frustrated by the attitudes he found prevalent in the publishing world. Oskison has too often been too casually dismissed by scholars, critics, and the general reading public. For a time he was all but forgotten. The publication of *The Singing Bird* by the University of Oklahoma Press has at least forestalled that unfortunate trend, and I congratulate the press for that.

My experiences with Pocketbooks and other publishers brought me close, in my own mind at least, to John Oskison. I felt as if I had picked up the banner to follow in his footsteps. I felt a tremendous sense of accomplishment when Pocketbooks began to publish my novels with Indians as main characters: *Go-Ahead Rider* and its two sequels, *Ned Christie's War*, *Crazy Snake*, *Captain Dutch*, and others. I felt as if John Oskison and I together had won a major battle.

Cherokee Cards

Since 1971, cards have become incredibly important to Cherokees. That was the year in which Cherokees were allowed to vote again in Cherokee Nation elections. In order to vote, however, one had to show descent from an ancestor on the Dawes Roll. Having met that requirement, the applicant would receive a blue card that read in part, "Cherokee Nation of Oklahoma: Notice of Registration to Vote." A few years later, registered Cherokees were told that we all had to re-register, and the re-registration process included getting a Certificate of Degree of Indian Blood (CDIB) issued by the U.S. Department of the Interior. Registration rather than enrollment was called for because the U.S. Congress had closed the Cherokee roll in 1914 and declared it to be the final Cherokee roll. When President Nixon and the U.S. Congress returned elections to the Cherokees in 1970, they neglected to bother with the closed Cherokee roll. I was a troublemaker. I wrote a letter protesting that I could not be removed as a tribal member once I had been accepted, and therefore I did not need to re-register. The answer I received was that I had never been a tribal member. I was merely a registered voter. I have always found it amusing that nonmembers of the tribe voted for the first chief and the first council members.

After that re-registration process, Cherokees (most of them) began carrying two cards: a Cherokee Nation registration card and a CDIB. And many Cherokees have come to believe that no one can be a Cherokee without those cards. Cards make the man or woman. When the American Indian Arts and Crafts Act of 1990 took effect, the Cherokee Nation suddenly turned its back on several artists it had been relying on for years because they did not have cards. Cherokee Nation hard-liners began saying of these artists and their offspring that they were not Cherokee.

Then there was the character I knew who told me that no one who did not have a card could claim to be Cherokee. He had a card. I asked him if he and his wife had a new child, would the child be Cherokee without a card? He said no. But once he went to the Cherokee Nation's registration office and did the necessary paperwork to get a card for the child, then the child would become Cherokee. That was the first time I realized that one could become Cherokee by processing paperwork. By the way, this same individual swore that a former employee of the Cherokee Nation who was a card carrier was a phony and was not really a Cherokee. He claimed that this man's cards were phonies. Is this doublethink?

The other point of view was provided by an old full-blood bilingual Cherokee man who was heard to say, "I don't need no got damn card to prove that I'm Indi'n."

The United Keetoowah Band of Cherokee Indians in Oklahoma, also a federally recognized tribe, used to enroll members in one of two ways. First, it used the same method as did the Cherokee Nation. That is, the applicant had to provide proof of descent from someone listed on the Dawes Roll. Unlike for the Cherokee Nation, however, the applicant also had to prove that he or she was at least one-quarter Cherokee. However, a Cherokee who did not have the proof, the paperwork required for all this process, could get the endorsement of a member of the Keetoowah band's council and be voted on by the council. In recent years, they have done away with that second method of enrollment and are going strictly by the first and, like the Cherokee Nation, are requiring a CDIB.

Voters have to show their cards in order to vote. Artists must show their cards in order to enter art shows. An artist identifying himself on a label underneath a painting or a piece of sculpture or a basket as Cherokee must show his Cherokee cards or be subject to a heavy fine under the 1990 law. (It's interesting that the makers of Jeeps can slap the word "Cherokee" on their product at will and not be bothered. Also a shoe manufacturing company and who knows what else?) Students have to show their cards in order to receive financial assistance. Cherokee cards and CDIBs are being flashed everywhere you turn.

It can work to the advantage of a quick-thinking Indian. A Cherokee friend of mine was driving an old man back to a reservation in Arizona, and the old man died en route. My friend was stopped on the highway for something or other, and the cop saw the body in the back of the van. "Is that guy dead?" he asked. My friend pulled out his CDIB and said, "Yes. This is my Department of Interior I.D. I'm taking him back to the reservation for burial." He got away with it.

One time in Billings, Montana, two Indian friends of mine and I took two foreign journalists out on the town. We were sitting in a bar and talking, and something led to the topic of how much Indian each of us was. We all recited off our degrees of Indian blood, the last of us, Richard King, saying, "I'm 29/32 Assiniboine Indian and the rest fur trapper." The two journalists looked at one another horrified, and one of them said, "We have never heard of anyone keeping pedigrees on human beings except Nazi Germany."

I do not have a CDIB. I thought that I was a member of the Cherokee Nation without one until I found out that I was only a registered voter. After that I enrolled in the Keetoowah Band. Then they changed their procedures. They have not yet told me that I've been un-Indianed yet again, but it could happen. Let them do their worst. I'm not applying for a CDIB. I could. My sister has, and she has received hers. My parents' and grandparents' CDIBs are the same as hers.

But here is the final irony of all this. The Cherokee Nation, defending its action in the March 3, 2007, vote to exclude the freedmen from the Cherokee membership list, said that it was determining its own membership. I say, "Bullshit." The Dawes Roll was prepared by the federal government, not by the Cherokee Nation, and the Cherokee Nation is still using that, or a part of it. And it is requiring CDIBs. Those are also provided by the U.S. government. Who is it that is determining the membership of the Cherokee Nation? Do you have a card?

Keetoowah

Keetoowah, according to Cherokee tradition, is the first Cherokee town. It is the mother town, the town from which all Cherokees originated, the town from which all other Cherokee towns developed. It was located in what is now western North Carolina. The site of Keetoowah is once again owned by Cherokees, the Eastern Band of Cherokees having purchased it in 1992. The original mound at the center of Keetoowah is still visible. I was taken to Keetoowah by my good friend Tom Belt, an Oklahoma Cherokee who has lived in Cherokee, North Carolina, now for several years. It was an awe-inspiring experience to be there where we all came from. Cherokees used to, and sometimes still do, call themselves Anikituwagi, or "People of Keetoowah." As time passed and the population grew, some people would move out from Keetoowah and establish new towns. The name has been spelled in various ways over the years: Kituwah, Katuah, Gituwah, and certainly some others that don't come to mind just now. Keetoowah is the most widely accepted spelling currently.

At sometime in history, a Keetoowah Society was born. Some Cherokees say that it is an ancient society that has just about always been with us. Although some Cherokees disagree with them, most scholars say that it was organized in what is now Oklahoma during or just before the Civil War, at the instigation of or with the help of Evan Jones (assisted by his son, John), a Baptist missionary and an abolitionist. Jones was eventually run out of the Cherokee Nation because of his abolitionist activities.

Whatever the truth of the origin of the Keetoowah Society, we certainly know more about it from those Civil War days. According to Georgia Rae Leeds in *The United Keetoowah Band of Cherokee*

154

Indians in Oklahoma, "The Keetoowahs believed that the impending Civil War threatened their tribal government; therefore, a group, encouraged by Baptist missionaries, John and Evan Jones, came together to save the purity of their customs and traditions."[1]

The Keetoowah Society was a secret society, and members took to wearing a pair of crossed pins under their coat lapels to identify one another. Because of that, during the Civil War they became known as the Pin Indians. They also came to be known as the Union Indians because of their opposition to the Confederacy, but they were likely much more concerned with the future of the Cherokee Nation than with the success of the Union. Even when Principal Chief John Ross signed a treaty with the Confederacy, many, if not most, of the Pin Indians refused to fight for the South. Ross, arrested by the Union and taken out of the Cherokee Nation, repudiated the treaty.

The Keetoowahs split in 1901 when Redbird Smith left the Keetoowah Society, along with a number of traditionalists, because the Keetoowahs were becoming political. Redbird's group became known as the Nighthawks or Nighthawk Keetoowahs. Today, both the Keetoowahs and Nighthawks are primarily religious and traditionalist in nature.

When the U.S. government all but demolished the Cherokee Nation with Oklahoma statehood in 1907, the Keetoowah Society was the only government for Cherokees in the new state. The United States, of course, did not recognize the Keetoowah government. Eventually, following the passage of the Oklahoma Indian General Welfare Act by the U.S. Congress in 1936, some of the Keetoowahs got together and formed a government that could be recognized and legalized under that act. They formed the United Keetoowah Band of Cherokee Indians in Oklahoma (UKB), made application through the Bureau of Indian Affairs, and in 1946 were officially recognized. The UKB is therefore a federally recognized Indian tribe, headquartered in Tahlequah, Oklahoma. At the time the UKB was recognized, the Cherokee Nation was just barely functioning. From time to time, the president of the United States appointed someone principal chief of the Cherokee Nation in order to have someone to sign some land transfer papers. Once the papers were signed, the "chief" would be unappointed. These men were known as "chiefs for a day." In 1941, J. B. Milam was appointed, and he remained in office for the rest of his life. Though the days of the "chiefs for a day" were gone at last, the Cherokee Nation still did not have elections. It did not have a tribal council. It had only an appointed principal chief. The UKB was therefore the only functioning tribal government for Cherokees in Oklahoma.

In 1970, the U.S. Congress, urged on by President Richard Nixon, returned elections to the Cherokee Nation, and W. W. Keeler, who had been the appointed chief since the death of Milam, was elected chief. He set about forming a tribal council again and having a new constitution approved. All of a sudden, Cherokees in Oklahoma had two tribal governments. The Cherokee Nation would (and still does) register for tribal membership anyone who can prove direct descent from someone on the Dawes Roll. The UKB requires one-quarter degree of Cherokee blood. For a time, the UKB did not require the kind of documentation the Cherokee Nation requires. A person lacking the paperwork could be vouched for by the tribal council. That has changed, however. Today, in order to be enrolled in the UKB, a person must prove descent from someone on the Dawes Roll and prove one-quarter degree of Cherokee blood.

For years after its organization and recognition, it seemed as if the UKB was struggling and would never get anywhere. In the 1970s, it got into a "cold war" with the Cherokee Nation. That war escalated when the UKB issued licenses to some members to operate smoke shops, and the Cherokee Nation, claiming exclusive jurisdiction over the land, declared the UKB smoke shops illegal and confiscated the cigarettes. There were threats of violence, but fortunately nothing came of them.

The UKB then opened a casino, which the Cherokee Nation tried time and again to shut down, but to no avail. The casino is still in full operation, bringing much-needed cash into the tribal coffers. Today, the UKB is operating a variety of tribal programs, including Cherokee language classes, an economic development authority, a tribal victim assistance program, a family services department, and an elder assistance program, and they sell tribal car tags. *Keetoowah News*, the official publication of the UKB, publishes news and regular council meeting minutes. The current UKB chief is bilingual Cherokee George Wickliffe.

The Dragging Canoe–
Nancy Ward Controversy

In 1776, Dragging Canoe was preparing to attack the illegal Watauga settlements on Cherokee land. The white settlers, known as Wataugans, had moved into the area in 1768 or 1769, and the Cherokees had warned them to move more than once over the seven or eight years of their occupancy. Henry Stuart, brother of John Stuart, British superintendent of Southern Indian Affairs, known to the Cherokees as Bushyhead, had written to the Wataugans requesting that they move out of Cherokee country. They refused. Dragging Canoe was out of patience with them. He planned his attack.

Dragging Canoe was opposed in his plan by his sister or cousin (depending on who you choose to believe), Nancy Ward. They argued both privately and publicly. Upon determining that Dragging Canoe was adamant in his determination to attack the settlements, Nancy Ward went to the traders Thomas, Williams, and Fawling, and told them of her kinsman's plans. She told them to warn the white people, and she helped sneak them away from the Cherokee town to accomplish their purpose.

The three traders were successful, and as a result, the whites were ready and waiting. Dragging Canoe was shot through his thighs. Others were wounded as well, and thirteen were killed.

The earliest popular interpretation of these events was that of Grace Steele Woodward in her history, *The Cherokees*, published in 1963. A popular book, it went through ten printings at the University of Oklahoma Press. Woodward says that Dragging Canoe was a hothead who hated white people and led savage forces. On the other hand, Nancy Ward, "known to be a friend to both whites and Indians . . . desired to avert bloodshed and save the lives of her people as well as those of the settlers." She was a "red paci-fist." In other words, Woodward's view led to a widely held view that lasted for a number of years that said that Dragging Canoe was a hostile savage, and Nancy Ward was a peaceful friend of white people. This interpretation surely helped to develop the curious fact that there seems to be among mostly "white Chero-kees" dozens and dozens of descendants of Nancy Ward and no descendants of Dragging Canoe.

In recent years the tables have turned. It did not take long for people of reasonable intelligence to look at the facts of recorded history and say, "Wait a minute. Nancy Ward got some of her own people killed, and the people she warned were actually squatters." Dragging Canoe had every right to attack the Watauga settlements. They had been warned by Cherokees and by the British govern-ment. Dragging Canoe was a patriot. Nancy Ward was a traitor. This became the popular stance for a time.

But let's take yet another look at the situation. The Cherokee Nation was in the middle of a painful and confusing period of transition. It was a matrilineal (not matriarchal) society. It was a society with definite roles for men and for woman. There was a male government out front and visible and a female government behind the scenes, so to speak. Women certainly had a voice in decision making, and Nancy Ward, known as the Ghigau (possibly Giga Agehya, Red Woman), or Beloved Woman, probably the highest political position a woman could achieve, had a right to at least have her voice heard. And Dragging Canoe was not listening.

During the Cherokee siege of Fort Loudoun in February 1760, just six years before the conflict between Dragging Canoe and Nancy Ward, some of the men in the fort were said to have had Cherokee wives or sweethearts who furnished them with food on the sly. When the women were discovered by the war chief, Oconos-tota, and chastised for this, they responded, "the soldiers were their husbands and it was their duty to help them."[1] The women were obviously not afraid to voice their opinions or to act according to their consciences. They knew their place. They knew their rights.

Six years later, Dragging Canoe was apparently ignoring the advice of a woman who not only was his sister or cousin but was the Beloved Woman. Probably he should have listened to her. When he had a son, the boy was called Young Dragging Canoe. That was contrary to Cherokee practices, as the boy belonged to his mother's clan and should have been given a clan name by an old woman of the clan.

Perhaps the clash between Dragging Canoe and Nancy Ward is but a reflection of the larger clash between the sexes, of the time when Cherokee men were taking rights that had not been theirs traditionally but which they had seen white men exercising, and when Cherokee women were trying to hold on to what had been their rights for countless generations. There were mixed-blood families among the Cherokees, many of them by this time, and in these families the white men acted as heads of household. The white men gave their surnames to their entire family. The entire Cherokee family structure was being turned upside down, and Nancy Ward knew that.

She certainly knew it by 1781 when she addressed the Cherokee National Council and a U.S. Treaty Commission, saying, "You know that women are always looked upon as nothing." In five years she had recognized defeat.

California Cherokees

California Cherokees are a pain in the ass. There are so damn many of them that before every Cherokee Nation election, those candidates who can afford to do so make a trip out to California to court them for their votes. That's expensive. It's time consuming. It takes time away from important campaigning at home in Oklahoma. It also angers many Cherokee people in Oklahoma that so many people who do not live in the boundaries of the Cherokee Nation are able to control the Cherokee Nation elections. Did I say control the elections? Yes, I did. I don't have the facts and figures, but it is widely believed that absentee voters actually do control Cherokee Nation elections. Of course, not all absentee voters are in California. There are Cherokees everywhere. But the vast majority, it seems, are in California. According to Russell Thornton in *The Cherokees: A Population History*, "There were 51,394 Cherokees in California in 1980."[1] Most Cherokees believe that most of the absentee voters are in California. It's probably true. How the hell did they get out there, and why?

It might surprise some people to find out that the first major migration of Cherokees to California occurred in 1849 and the years immediately after with the California gold rush. Cherokees were among the '49ers! Some famous Cherokees made the trip seeking their fortune. John Rollin Ridge, son of the slain treaty signer John Ridge, made the trip in 1850. He was not necessarily seeking his fortune, or at least that may only have been a secondary reason. Ridge had killed a man in the Cherokee Nation, and he believed that the administration of Chief John Ross would seek to hang him for murder. He was running for his life.

When he got to California, however, he tried his hand at gold mining. He had little success. He turned to journalism instead, working for several different newspapers. He also became a popular and widely read poet, and he wrote a novel, *The Life and Adventures of Joaquin Murieta, the Celebrated California Bandit.* Although Ridge expressed his desire to return home to the Cherokee Nation over and again, he never did, dying in Grass Valley, California, in 1867. (There are some California Cherokees today, living in Sacramento, who are still taking care of his grave.)

Ridge's relatives, John A. Watie and Charles Watie, brothers of Stand Watie, also made the long and arduous journey to California. Edward W. (Ned) Bushyhead went to California as well. Like Ridge, he tried gold mining for a time but eventually turned to journalism, where he was quite successful. However, he achieved fame as a lawman. He remained in California until his death. Ned's brother, Dennis Wolfe Bushyhead, went also, but he returned to the Cherokee Nation later to be elected principal chief in 1879.

John Watie described the trip in a letter to his brother Stand. He said that the trip had been 3,000 miles long, and he had been "on the road six months and ten days." E. Raymond Evans wrote an article on these Cherokee gold seekers called "Following the Rainbow: The Cherokees in the California Gold Fields."[2] He mentioned not only John Rollin Ridge and John Watie, but several others: Barbara Longknife, D. Jarrett Bell, Clement McNair, Bug Eye Smith, Sinacowee, and Chap England. There were others: Johnson Thompson and Colonel Oliver Hazard Perry Brewer, for example. Some returned to the Cherokee Nation. Some remained in California. Thornton says that only 258 Cherokees were in California in 1930. That was about to change though.

When the Great Depression hit hard, 12,000 Cherokees left their homes in Oklahoma and went to California. They went for the same reasons other Americans from the heartland went. They were looking for jobs in the land of milk and honey.

In the 1950s, the federal government's relocation program sent many Cherokees once again to California. Wilma Mankiller's family was one of those. Wilma returned to the Cherokee Nation in 1977. She became principal chief in 1985. Several of my wife's aunts and uncles on her mother's side of the family made the move. Some have returned to Oklahoma in recent years. Some are still out there.

In addition to the three major migrations of Cherokees to California, individual Cherokees have made the move for their own reasons. Will Rogers had made the move as early as 1919. He had starred in his first movie, filmed in New Jersey, and then had been offered a lucrative film contract, so he moved to California, and he stayed. Carl Davis Matthews, Cherokee from Oklahoma, was in Los Angeles in the 1930s working as a stunt double and playing villains in B western movies, often under the professional name Cherokee Matthews. He remained active in Cherokee politics and causes, but he stayed in California for the rest of his life, dying there in 1959.

Clu Gulager located in Los Angeles to pursue a film and television career in the 1950s. He retired from acting, but he has remained in Los Angeles. Wes Studi made the same move in the 1980s, but once he met with success, he made the sensible decision of relocating to Santa Fe, New Mexico.

I have made trips to California to the Los Angeles area for book signings, where I have been hosted by Cherokee friends out there, but so far I have showed the good sense and restraint to always return to Oklahoma. I have long been aware of the indisputable fact that residence in California leads inevitably to madness. On the other hand, it seems to me that since there are so many California Cherokees, and since they are so far removed from all three federally recognized Cherokee tribes, they might be well served to organize and petition the Bureau of Indian Affairs for federally recognized status themselves and become a separate tribe, the fourth federally recognized Cherokee tribe in the United States.

Tribally Specific Historical Fiction

Much of my writing over the years has been historical fiction. More to the point, it has been what I call tribally specific historical fiction, or to be brief, tribal historical fiction. As far as I know, I'm the first writer to use that description for my work, but I'm certainly not the first to write the kind of material I'm concerned with here. John Oskison's novel *The Singing Bird* is such a work. But let me begin with some definitions.

There's a wide range of historical fiction. I suppose one of the first titles to come to mind for most folks, especially students of European literature, is *War and Peace*. And for a long time, Tolstoy's masterpiece provided the basic structure of what was called historical fiction. The novel takes as its background the invasion of Russia by Napoleon's army, and Napoleon and other historical characters appear in the novel as minor characters, but the main characters in the story are fictional ones. The writer is saying to his readers, "This is how ordinary people might have been affected by these major historical events."

The pattern has been used over and over again, notably by Edna Ferber in such novels as *Cimarron* and *Ice Palace*. General Lew Wallace used it in *Ben Hur*. I used it in *Mountain Windsong*, my novel about the Cherokee Trail of Tears. In these novels, the main characters are fictional, but the historical background is accurate, at least reasonably so.

But since there are no rules in literature, and literary categories are the creation of booksellers and librarians and critics, historical fiction has taken other paths since Tolstoy's *War and Peace*. Robert Graves's *I, Claudius* is a fine example of a novel in which the main historical players are also the main characters in the book. And I've followed that path as well in novels like *The Saga of Henry Starr*, *Ned Christie's War*, and *Zeke Proctor: Cherokee Outlaw*.

Some might go so far as to say that any novel set in an earlier period than that in which it was written is historical fiction in that, though its plot and characters are fictional, it reflects an earlier time. Therefore *Shane* is a historical novel—or a piece of historical fiction. And my own three *Go-Ahead Rider* novels might also fall under that definition.

Then there are those books wherein the writer has taken all kinds of liberties with history and seems to have mixed up all of the above approaches. A prime recent example of this kind of careless approach to history is (choke—I don't like to say or write that name—I usually choke on it) Larry McMurtry's *Zeke and Ned*. McMurtry and his cowriter, Dianne Osanna, took two Cherokee historical personages, Zeke Proctor and Ned Christie, and combined their two stories to make one long "historical novel." They exaggerated the violence and made no attempt at understanding and therefore accurately depicting Cherokee character, Cherokee culture, or Cherokee beliefs. The novel shows no evidence of the writers having made any attempt at discovering what the Cherokee Nation of the time was like. When called on these and other points, their defense was, "We called it fiction." In my opinion, novels like *Zeke and Ned* use the label "historical fiction" as an excuse for sloppy writing.

This brings me to my personal first and main rule, or guiding principle, in writing historical fiction, and that is to make the representation of the times, places, and characters as accurate as possible. That does not mean that every detail must be included or that the novel must be footnoted and documented, heaven forbid.

During the American Revolution, a time in which Dragging Canoe was very active on the side of the British, there were dozens, possibly hundreds of raids back and forth between the Cherokees and the backwoods American settlers. Obviously, a novel cannot include them all. And we do not know exactly who took part in all these raids. As a writer of fiction, I have to include descriptions of some of them. If there are no detailed historical descriptions available, I have to invent them, but in doing so, I try to make my description as historically accurate as possible. That is to say, based on available descriptions of other fights of the times, I try to describe one as it might have happened.

Here's another example of the kind of decision that one faces writing historical fiction. Some years ago I wrote a novel called *Ned Christie's War*. There are several photographs of Ned Christie, and in all of them, he's dressed casually and his hair is long, hanging halfway to his waist. After Christie was killed by a federal posse, they propped up his body and took a photograph. He's wearing a suit, and his hair is short. I could have ignored those facts. All historians who have dealt with Ned Christie have done so. But I wanted to deal with them in some way. They were bothering me. The man was at home expecting an attack. Why did he put on a suit? And why, after a lifetime of wearing his hair long, did he cut it? Finally my wife, Evelyn, who grew up in a conservative Cherokee setting, suggested the following scene to me, and it is in the novel. The setting is in the late 1800s, in the Cherokee Nation, Indian Territory, shortly before Oklahoma statehood.

Ned walked to the stove and checked the pan there. There was still hot coffee. He got a cup, poured himself some, and carried it to the table. He sat down and was reaching for a piece of the good corn bread there when he heard the dogs. It was not a menacing bark, as if the dogs had sensed some intruder in their territory. It was not the deep-throated baying of the hounds on the trail of a rabbit or a raccoon or some other creature of the woods. Rather it was a cacophony of whines and whimpers, accompanied by scratching at the door. These were not house dogs, had not ever, in fact, been inside the house. Ned turned to face the door. His face showed a calm resignation. Gatey and the two Archies also stopped still and listened. No one spoke. The two Archies looked at each other. Then Arch Christie looked up at his mother. She was staring at the door. Ned picked up the piece of corn bread he had reached for. He ate the corn bread and drank his coffee in silence. By the time he had finished, the dogs had stopped their whining and gone their ways. Ned stood up, walked to the door, opened it and went outside.

He walked into his shop, found the lantern in the dark, lit it and turned up the light. Then he found a pair of shears. He rejected them and found another pair. He tested their edge. Then he took them to his grinding stone and sharpened them. He tested their edge again. He reached back behind his head with his left hand and gathered up his long hair. Then with the shears in his right, he reached back to cut. Carefully he placed the shorn locks on a clean corner of his work table. Then he cut some more. . . . [Finally] he gathered up all the locks of hair he had cut from his head, and he folded them up in an oil cloth. He stuck the oil cloth inside his shirt and went to a corner of the shop for a shovel. With the shovel in one hand and the lantern in the other, he walked into the woods. He dug the hole deep, and down in the bottom of the hole, he placed the folded oil cloth containing the hair. He replaced the dirt, patted it down, smoothed it and covered it with leaves. Then he went to the creek. Back inside the house, later, Ned found that the others had already prepared everything. Well, almost everything. He got out his best suit and his white shirt, and he laid them out carefully. Gatey and the two Archies stared at Ned, briefly, a long stare would have been impolite. He looked quite a bit different with his hair cropped short. He looked somehow shorter and stockier. And he seemed to look a different age. Was it older or younger? They couldn't decide. He looked different. No one said anything, not about the dogs, not about the hair.

I recently finished work on a novel based on the life of Sequoyah. When I was trying to get started, I made the frustrating discovery that virtually everything about this remarkable man is controversial. Gathering all the information I could from historians and biographers, I learned that Sequoyah was born anywhere from 1760 to

1780, and in spite of the fact that his death is fairly well documented, there's even a two-year discrepancy there. He was crippled, walked with a limp, either from a childhood disease, from a youthful accident, or from a war wound. He had anywhere from one to five wives, anywhere from two to twenty children. And finally, he may or may not have actually invented the Cherokee syllabary. Almost everything I wrote in *Sequoyah* was a result of weighing all the different opinions and then trying to determine which of them made the most sense. Here is a brief scene from that novel

Sequoyah did not often lose his temper, so Sally was surprised when he came storming into the house one afternoon. She could tell right away that he'd been drinking again. He stumbled over to the table, sat down heavily, dropping his cane to the floor, and slammed his fist down on the tabletop.

"What's wrong with you?" she asked him.

"That David Brown," Sequoyah said.

"The young man who worked with Reverend Washburn?"

"Yes. That one."

"I thought he had gone back to the old country."

"He only went back for a visit, but now he's back here. There's a new white preacher back in the old country. They called him Woostah or something like that. David Brown is working with him now. He has already translated much of the white preacher's book into our language by using my symbols. And they're going to order type and a printing press. They mean to put the whole book into my symbols. I wish I had never made them."

"You shouldn't say that, Sequoyah," Sally said. "You spent years working on the writing. You put up with much abuse for it, even from me. But now our people can read and write in our own language. Almost everyone. You should be proud of what you've done."

"The preachers tell everyone that everything we believe in is wrong. Then they tell them that what it says in their book is right. Now it seems, I've given them a new weapon in this fight. I wish I had never done it."

Just about everything I read about Sequoyah indicated to me that he would have felt that way about the missionaries and their work. He would have felt that way about the use to which his syllabary was being put.

So far I've been talking about historical fiction in a rather general way, but my topic here is tribal historical fiction, and I believe that what distinguishes tribal historical fiction from any other historical fiction is simply the point of view. By that I don't mean that tribal historical fiction is just historical fiction written by a Native American writer. What I mean is that tribal historical fiction is written from a point of view that comes from within the specific tribal culture. Tribal historical fiction should express the views of the tribal people involved. If a Lakota writes about the Little Big Horn fight, his or her point of view will be much different from a discussion written by a white author. If a Cherokee writes about Dragging Canoe's alliance with the British during the American Revolution, his or her point of view will be very different from that of an American patriot writing about the war. That much is obvious.

But I think that still more is involved in writing from a point of view from within a culture. The various Native American tribal belief systems are vastly different from anything in the European or Euro-American experience. To say that something is written from a tribal point of view is to say, I believe, that it is written from a point of view that totally accepts that tribal belief system.

Shakespeare's *Hamlet* is written from a point of view of a Renaissance Englishman. In that belief system, a man is bound to avenge the murder of his father. He is bound to avenge the murder of his king. But the murderer of Hamlet's father has become the king, and it is certain damnation to kill the king. That is Hamlet's dilemma, and without an understanding of that dilemma, the play becomes nothing more than the wishy-washy, namby-pamby tale of a man who cannot make up his mind.

In *Mountain Windsong*, I wrote, "I was looking straight up into the sky, and I tried to imagine what it was like on the other side. Grandpa had told me that it was a gigantic vault over the earth—kind of like a cereal bowl turned upside-down over a saucer—and we were walking around on the saucer under the bowl."

Anything claiming to have been written from a traditional Cherokee tribal point of view, I believe, must include that cosmic view. In *The Way of the Priests*, when I might have written, "The Sun was coming up," I wrote instead, "At long last he saw some light in the eastern sky along the horizon. The Sun had completed her journey across the top of the Sky Vault and had re-emerged in the east on the underside." It's important to note, I think, that the novel does not say, "he believed" or "he thought." It says "the Sun" had done all that.

Here's another passage from that same novel. "He would consult his *uluhsadi*, the rare and valuable transparent crystal taken from the forehead of the *ukitena*, the great anomalous creature from the chaotic underworld, and the crystal would show him the way." Again, I did not say, "the crystal he believed had come from the forehead of a mythological creature." I said that it had come from there.

Wili Woyi—in English, Billy Pigeon—is remembered by Oklahoma Cherokees today as one of the greatest of all Cherokee medicine men. Toward the end of the nineteenth century, Wili Woyi was accused of murder by federal authorities and pursued for something like eleven years. Historians tell us that when the lawmen got to his home, he would be away. Cherokees tell a very different tale. Here's a scene from my short story "Wili Woyi."

Glenn Colvert was approaching the home of Wili Woyi for the second time in less than a week, but this time he was not alone. With him rode Harper Monk and Birk Estey, both deputies from Fort Smith assigned by Moss Berman to ride with and assist Colvert in the arrest of Billy Pigeon. Berman considered a man who was wanted for murder and had already escaped once from an experienced deputy to be a serious enough threat to merit additional manpower. It had been a source of embarrassment to Colvert, but as he had lost his prisoner, there was not much he could say. Usually a loud talkative man, Colvert had been unusually quiet the whole way from Fort Smith to Muskogee by rail and thence on horseback with Monk and Estey.

Just before the point in their journey at which Wili Woyi's cabin would become visible to them, Colvert reined in his mount and called a halt.

"Now, boys," he said, "of course, we ain't got no way of knowing if Pigeon's at home or not, but let's not take no chances. He's sneaky as hell. Believe me. I know. Now, what I suggest we do is I think you two had ought to spread out and go through the woods so one of you comes up on each side of the house. You can cover the back as well as the front that way. I'll give you time to get in position, then I'll move in on the front. I'll call out to him first. Give him a chance to come out peaceable. But if he takes out the back, you all cut down on him right quick. If he don't come out neither door, then I'll move on in."

It took only a few minutes for Monk and Estey to position themselves, and when Colvert was sure that they had had enough time, he stepped out into the open facing Wili Woyi's cabin, rifle in hand.

"Pigeon," he shouted. "Bill Pigeon."

Then aloud, but only to himself, he muttered, "Seems as how I've been here before."

"Bill Pigeon. You in there?"

The only sounds to answer him were the gentle rustling of the breeze through the giant oaks and walnuts, the scamperings of busy squirrels, the flight of some crows, and, off in the distance, the rapid rat-tat-tat of a woodpecker hard at work. Colvert began moving toward the cabin. Slowly. Cautiously. About halfway across the clearing which lay before the cabin, Colvert let his eyes dart rapidly from one side of the cabin to the other. There were no outbuildings in sight. The only place that looked as if it might be used to shelter animals was a depression in the rock behind the cabin and to Colvert's left. It looked as if it might accommodate two or three horses, but that was about all. It was not too deep though, and although it was heavily in shadow, Colvert could see that Wili Woyi's horse was not there. He stopped when he reached the door, paused for an instant, then called out again. "Pigeon. You in there?"

There was no answer.

Colvert, his heart pounding, tried the door. It opened easily. He pushed it just a few inches, peering inside. There was dim light inside the cabin.

"Anybody home?"

Still no answer. Colvert shoved the door all the way inside to the wall to be sure that no one was lurking behind it. Then, with one foot across the threshold, he poked his nose inside and slowly looked around. He stepped back outside with a strange and eerie sense of relief.

"Monk. Birk. Come on out, boys. Ain't nobody home. God damn it."

As the three riders from Fort Smith disappeared back down the road by which they had come, inside the cabin Wili Woyi uncrossed his legs and rose to his feet. He walked straight across the room to the still open door, leaned with his left hand against the door frame and stared after his departing visitors. With his right hand he raised to his lips the cup of steaming coffee that he held and took a long and satisfying sip.

It's not a subtle difference, and the difference is not insignificant. It has everything to do with the point of view coming from within the culture. Without that point of view, we may be writing historical fiction, but we're not writing what I would call tribal historical fiction. The writer has to believe that there is a Sky Vault over us all, that the Sun crawls along the top at night and across the bottom in the daytime, that a medicine person really does divine from a crystal that was obtained from the forehead of the ukitena, and that Wili Woyi could actually make himself invisible. And if the writer believes strongly enough and has enough skill, the writer can make his or her readers believe it as well, at least for the time they are reading the book.

I do believe that tribal historical fiction has an important place in our contemporary society. It's important for all of us to have all people know that when Native American people fought, they were fighting for their land and for their way of life. They were, in fact, fighting invaders. It's also important for people to know just how those Native people felt about what was happening around them. Tribal historical fiction, historical fiction written from a specific tribal point of view, can go a long way toward providing that kind of knowledge to a large number of people. In addition, it lets Native people know that their literary traditions are alive and well and vital and still evolving.

Cherokees and Sports

Cherokees have always been damn near fanatical about sports, whether they are participating or observing. They shout and scream. They call the officials all kinds of horribly insulting names. They threaten. I don't know this for a fact, but I would bet that they've always been that way. In the old days, that is, the days before Cherokees were unduly influenced by white people, there were a number of ancient games Cherokees played. There was the ball game. There was chunkey. There was a hoop and pole game. There was racing, blowgun shooting, and archery. Cherokees almost always combined their love of these games with their love of gambling. And some of the games were much more important than just games.

If we can use the order of the tales as recorded in the cycle by James Mooney in *Myths of the Cherokee* as indicative, and if we can assume that the earliest mentioned games are the most important, then the ball game is first. The tale recorded by Mooney is in the cycle of animal tales, before human beings are present. Mooney calls it "The Ball Game of the Birds and Animals," and it goes like this.[1]

Once the animals challenged the birds to a great ballplay, and the birds accepted. The leaders made the arrangements and fixed the day, and when the time came both parties met at the place for the ball dance, the animals on a smooth grassy bottom near the river and the birds in the treetops over by the ridge. The captain of the animals was the Bear, who was so strong and heavy that he could pull down anyone who got in his way. All along the road to the ball ground he was tossing up great logs to show his strength and boasting of

174

what he would do to the birds when the game began. The Terrapin, too—not the little one we have now, but the great original Terrapin—was with the animals. His shell was so hard that the heaviest blows could not hurt him, and he kept rising up on his hind legs and dropping heavily again to the ground, bragging that this was the way he would crush any bird that tried to take the ball from him. Then there was the Deer, who could outrun every other animal. Altogether it was a fine company.

The birds had the Eagle for their captain, with the Hawk and the great Tla nuwa, all swift and strong of flight, but still they were a little afraid of the animals. The dance was over and they were all pruning their feathers up in the trees and waiting for the captain to give the word when here came two little things hardly larger than fieldmice climbing up the tree in which sat perched the bird captain. At last they reached the top, and creeping along the limb to where the Eagle captain sat they asked to be allowed to join in the game. The captain looked at them, and seeing that they were four footed, he asked why they did not go to the animals, where they belonged. The little things said that they had, but the animals had made fun of them and driven them off because they were so small. Then the bird captain pitied them and wanted to take them.

But how could they join the birds when they had no wings? The Eagle, the Hawk, and the others consulted, and at last it was decided to make some wings for the little fellows. They tried for a long time to think of something that might do, until someone happened to remember the drum they had used in the dance. The drumhead was of groundhog skin and maybe they could cut off a corner and make wings of it. So they took two pieces of leather from the drumhead and cut them into shape for wings, and stretched them with cane splints and fastened them on to the forelegs of one of the small animals, and in this way came Tla meha, the Bat. They threw the ball to him and told him to catch it, and by the way he dodged and circled about, keeping the ball always in the air and never letting it fall to the ground, the birds soon saw that he would be one of their best men.

Now they wanted to fix the other little animal, but they had used up all their leather to make wings for the Bat, and there was no time to send for more. Somebody said that they might do it by stretching his skin, so two large birds took hold from opposite sides with their strong bills, and by pulling at his fur for several minutes they managed to stretch the skin on each side between the fore and hind feet, until they had Tewa, the Flying Squirrel. To try him the bird captain threw up the ball, and the Flying Squirrel sprang off the limb after it, caught it in his teeth and carried it through the air to another tree nearly across the bottom.

When they were all ready the signal was given and the game began, but almost at the first toss the Flying Squirrel caught the ball and carried it up a tree, from which he threw it to the birds, who kept it in the air for some time until it dropped.

The Bear rushed to get it, but the Martin darted after it and threw it to the Bat, who was flying near the ground, and by his dodging and doubling kept it out of the way of even the Deer, until he finally threw it in between the posts and won the game for the birds.

The Bear and the Terrapin, who had boasted so of what they would do, never got a chance even to touch the ball. For saving the ball when it dropped, the birds afterwards gave the Martin a gourd in which to build his nest, and he still has it.

This first recorded instance of a Cherokee ball game doesn't really give us much idea of the game or how it is played. It does tell us that the ball was thrown between the posts for a score. It sounds like that one score was enough to win the game. Mooney says that the "ballplay" is called "*anetsa*" or "*anetsagi*" in Cherokee. In English, it is sometimes called stickball. Cherokees also called the ball game "the little brother of war." Charles Hudson, in *The Southeastern Indians*, says that the ball game season "began in mid-summer and lasted until it was too cold to play."[2]

Ritual observations surrounding the game were many and strict. A ball player could not eat rabbit meat because the rabbit is easily confused. He could not eat frog meat. The frog's bones are brittle. On the other hand, the ball player rubbed himself with eel skin, because it was slippery. Mooney says, "In preparing ball-players for the contest, the medicine man sometimes burns splinter of [wood from a lightning-struck tree] to coal, which he gives to the players to paint themselves with in order that they may be able to strike their opponents with all the force of a thunderbolt."[3] Ball players often had themselves ritually scratched in order to make them fast runners.

The game was played between two different towns, often between towns of different tribes. Sometimes, in addition to the many individual bets made on a game, huge wagers would be made. For instance, it was said that the Cherokees won a vast piece of land from the Creeks that way. However, there are actually some ambiguous historical references, for "ballplay" was also a figurative expression for the making of war, so if the Cherokees said of a parcel of land, "We won it from the Creeks playing ball," they might have won it playing ball or they might have won it in an actual battle.

On the night before a ball game, the town held a ball game dance. Women sang ball game songs. The men danced around a fire with their ballsticks in their hands. Seven women, representing the seven clans, danced near two upright poles representing the goal on the playing field. During the dance, a conjurer placed black beads representing the opposing players underneath a flat rock, and from time to time the women stomped on the rock. The men also called on spiritual help for the coming game. Much more ritual was associated with the game.

The next day, when the opposing team arrived, they were informed about exactly where the game would be played. The town had several different ball fields in order to confuse any conjurer the opposition might send to "doctor" the playing field.

When the two teams arrived at the playing field, there would be hundreds of spectators there already awaiting the game and placing their bets. The field itself, according to Hudson, could be anywhere from one hundred to five hundred yards long, and at each end it had two posts driven into the ground about three yards apart with a crosspiece at the top for the goals. Throwing the ball between the posts or striking one of the posts with the ball scored one point. In historic times, a game was won when one side had scored twelve points.

Players carried two ballsticks, two to two and a half feet long, bent into a loop at one end, which was laced with deerskin or some other appropriate material. The ball was made of deerskin and stuffed with deer or squirrel hair. It was a little larger than a contemporary golf ball. Play started when an old man walked onto the field and tossed the ball into the air between the two teams. The game could go on for several hours and was very rough indeed. Although Cherokees in Oklahoma abandoned the game, it has been played continuously by the Cherokees in North Carolina.

In 1975 or 1976, some young Cherokee men in Oklahoma decided to revive stickball. They put together a team and practiced, and then challenged the Eastern Cherokee team from Wolf Town, North Carolina, to a game. The Oklahoma Cherokees traveled to North Carolina for the game. When they returned home, after having been defeated, of course, they had broken bones and bruises. The Wolf Town players made the trip to Tahlequah the next year to play again against the Okies at the Cherokee National Holiday. Since they were the visitors, they were much kinder, winning the game but not inflicting any harm on the Okies.

I witnessed that game. I recall that the Wolf Town players had one large, heavy player on their side. I wondered what good he would be to them. He stood in the middle of the field watching the action, until he figured out who was the fastest player on the Oklahoma side. Eventually, that player ran too close to the heavy Wolf Town player, and that heavy player grabbed him and held him out of the remainder of the game. I also remember seeing a player from Wolf Town get the ball, drop his sticks, stuff the ball into his mouth, and run like hell until he made it between the goal posts. Spectators at these games must watch at their own risk, as there is no out of bounds. If the ball goes into the crowd, the players will follow.

After Oklahoma statehood, the ball game was outlawed in the new state, but Cherokees, being not only fiercely competitive but also very adaptable, shifted to baseball, softball, and basketball, baseball and softball being initially more popular because of the lack of basketball courts. Some Cherokee communities in Oklahoma have several baseball fields around, reflecting the old stickball practice. By the way, it is no longer illegal to play stickball in Oklahoma.

There is another version of stickball played by Cherokees. This one is played with men on one side and women on the other. Today it is played primarily following an all-night stomp dance. This game is played around a single pole with usually a carved fish on top. The pole has a hole drilled in it on the top, and the fish has a peg sticking down from its belly. The peg is inserted into the hole so that when the fish is struck by the ball, the fish spins. As in the larger ball game, the men use ballsticks. They are not allowed to touch the ball with their hands. The women, however, do not have sticks. They do use their hands. Not surprisingly, the women almost always win this game.

Another ancient and very important game for Cherokees was what Cherokees called gatayusti. It's better known today by its Creek name of chunkey. Like the "ballplay," the chunkey game was accompanied by heavy betting. The game itself was played with a long pole, like a spear, and a discoidal stone. Rodney Leftwich, in *Arts and Crafts of the Cherokee*, describes the stones: "These stone disks, five to six inches in diameter and about two inches thick, had concave sides and were sometimes pierced. They were made from quartzite, granite or other soft grained stone, were almost perfectly symmetrical and were highly polished."[4] The game was played by two men at a time. One man rolled the stone, and then both men flung their poles and ran after them. The game was scored by how close the stone was to various marks on the poles. This game is also prominent in an old tale recorded by Mooney, and I have retold that tale in my essay on Indian casinos in this volume. This game, still played during colonial times, was witnessed by James Adair, who described it in his book *History of the American Indians*, published in 1775. Somewhere along the way it was abandoned.

Hudson describes a Creek game called "rolling a stone," which was played by rolling a small ball "along a trench several feet long."[5] There were holes at the end of the trench, some more difficult to enter than others. This could be the game that developed into what is known today as "Cherokee marbles." Cherokee marbles was played in the 1890s, for Ned Christie was known to be a marble player. It is still played today in Cherokee communities in northeastern Oklahoma. The Cherokee name of the game is *digadayosdi*. The marbles are polished round stones about the size of billiard balls. In fact, players today often use billiard balls rather than go to the trouble of polishing their own marbles. The playing field is anywhere from 105 to 120 feet long, with holes in the ground every 35 to 40 feet. The first four holes are laid out in a straight line. The fifth is set off at a right angle from number four so that the lineup of holes forms an L shape. The game is played by two teams. Each member of each team tries to get his marble in each hole. When that has been achieved, he turns around to go back through the holes again. Players can use their marbles to knock opponents' marbles out of play. The first team to get all of its players' marbles back in hole number one is the winner. Hastings Shade, former deputy principal chief of the Cherokee Nation, is one of the few remaining marble makers.

Cherokees have always been fond of foot racing, and, of course, they bet on the races. A foot race is detailed in a story recorded by Mooney called "Ga'na's Adventures." In this story, the first race was run without betting. In the second race, bets were made. The third race was longer than the first two, and bets were made on that one as well. But the first story involving a race is in the animal tales as recorded by Mooney, which he calls "How the Terrapin Beat the Rabbit." It's more widely known as one of Uncle Remus's tales. It's the story of how the Terrapin won a race against the Rabbit. In the version recorded by Mooney, the Terrapin wins by cheating. Since all Terrapins look alike, he has his relatives hidden out along the race course, and when Rabbit is not looking, one of the Terrapins up ahead moves out onto the track. In the better-known version, the cocky Rabbit lies down to take a nap and fails to wake up. The Terrapin overtakes him and wins the race. The notorious Tom Starr, said to have killed one hundred men in retaliation for the killing of his father, was also said to have been a great foot racer. Andy Payne won the first International Transcontinental Foot Race from Ascot Park in Los Angeles to Madison Square Garden in New York City, in 1928, running a total of 3,422.3 miles in 573 hours, 4 minutes, and 34 seconds, over a period of eighty-four days.

I know nothing about any competition in the early Cherokee days involving the blowgun or bow and arrows, but both are featured in the activities of the Cherokee National Holiday these days. And Sampson Owl, chief of the Eastern Band from 1923 until 1927, is said to have been able to hit a six-foot-square target at one hundred feet with a dart from his blowgun. The archery competition today is called the "corn stalk shoot," because the target is a bundle of corn stalks. During the holiday, there is traditional archery competition and modern bow competition. Joe Thornton, a Cherokee, was a great champion archer in the days before archery became an Olympic sport, winning the Oklahoma state championship in 1960, winning a gold medal at the U.S. archery competition and setting three world records in 1961, winning the British National Championship in 1962, winning a silver medal at the world archery championships in 1963, and winning the U.S. National Championship in 1970.

My cousin, John Conley, is a world-class championship marksman with black powder guns, both long and short. He shoots old Remington and Colt revolvers, Henry and Winchester rifles, and long-barreled flintlock and caplock rifles. He has an incredible collection of trophies, having won competitions in Arkansas, Oklahoma, and Texas over any number of years.

Will Rogers was an avid roper and polo player, and some of his relatives, including Clem McSpadden, continue that tradition. Eastern Band Cherokee chief Osley Bird Saunooke (1951–55 and 1959–63) was a professional wrestler before turning to politics. He started wrestling in 1937, and at six feet six inches tall and weighing

369 pounds, he became the super heavyweight champion of the world, holding the title for fourteen years. He retired from wrestling in 1951. Wilson Vann is one of the top teachers and practitioners of the martial arts, holding a black belt in kodokan judo and a sixth degree black belt in tae kwon do. With over thirty years experience, he now operates a martial arts school in Tahlequah, and he has taken his students to Korea for competition.

Lillian Justice played basketball for Tahlequah High School and was so good that her number was retired and her uniform placed on display for years. After high school, she attended Tulsa Business College where she played Amateur Athletic Union (AAU) basketball for its team, the Tulsa Stenos. When she went to work at the American National Insurance Company in Houston, Texas, she played for its AAU team, the Anicas, when they won the AAU National Championship twice. She was named all-American six times. She retired from sports following an injury in 1938. Joe Byrd, former principal chief of the Cherokee Nation, went to Northeastern State University on a basketball scholarship. Another Cherokee basketball player nearly twenty years later was Gene Conley, but I'll mention him more below under baseball.

Sonny Sixkiller was quarterback for the University of Washington beginning in 1970. He was named to the Huskies Hall of Fame in 1975, and he went on to play professional football briefly for Toronto in the Canadian Football League and then in the World Football League for Philadelphia and for Hawaii. Sammy Jack Claphan played football for the Stilwell High School Indians, then for the University of Oklahoma, and then professionally for the San Diego Chargers.

Austin Ben Tincup pitched for the Philadelphia Phillies in 1914. In 1917, he moved to the Little Rock Travelers (Arkansas), and in 1928 he went to Chicago. He was inducted into the American Indian Athletic Hall of Fame in 1981.

Gene Conley, originally from Muskogee, has been called one of the greatest athletes of all time. He went to Washington State University where he played both basketball and baseball. He started playing professional baseball in 1952 for the Boston Braves. In 1957, he was with the Milwaukee Braves when they won the

World Series. He also played for the Boston Red Sox and the Philadelphia Phillies. At the same time he played professional baseball, he played professional basketball, first for the Boston Celtics and then for the New York Knicks. While playing for the Celtics, he was on their championship teams in 1959, 1960, and 1961. Thus Gene became the only professional athlete to have championship rings in two different professional sports.

Dan Robbins (known in later years as W. Lee and then as Mr. W.) played professional baseball for Gene Autry's Los Angeles Angels beginning in 1961 for two seasons. He was a pitcher.

Cherokees have produced a good many outstanding sports figures, but the real subject of this essay is the near fanaticism of all Cherokees when it comes to sports. The Cherokee Nation's Sequoyah High School has football, baseball, girl's slow-pitch softball, boys' basketball, girls' basketball, wrestling, and track. All events are well attended by vocal fans. The sports page of a recent issue of the *Cherokee Phoenix* carried nearly two pages of color photographs and stories about the Lady Indians basketball team winning their third straight Class 3A title. Another story was about the boys' basketball team just missing the tournament win. And there were stories about the track team, the baseball team, the girls' softball team, and the wrestling team, and one about a Cherokee who was a football player for Northeastern State University being inducted into the university's Athletic Hall of Fame. The Sequoyah students are a minority of the total number of Cherokee students. There are high schools all over the Cherokee Nation, which includes all or parts of fourteen counties of northeastern Oklahoma. All of the schools have teams, and Cherokee students play on them all. All of them have fiercely loyal fans.

But the amazing thing is that there are dozens of independent baseball teams, men's and women's and boys' and girls' slow-pitch softball and fast-pitch softball teams, and basketball teams all over Cherokee country for Cherokees of all ages. These teams do not stop when Cherokees are out of high school. Little League be damned. These teams just keep on going. They are for people going to college or not going to college, working or not working, who just still want to play ball. Anyone can put together a team and look for sponsors to help pay for uniforms, equipment, transportation, and other expenses connected to traveling to and from out-of-town games and tournaments, and entry fees for the tournaments. The coaches and managers of these teams travel around the Cherokee country looking for likely prospects to recruit, and they steal players from one another.

These independent teams have been around for a long time. My wife's father, Swimmer Wesley Snell, Adawosgi, played for them. He was born in 1899 and died in 1972. When he was a lad, he was ritually scratched to make him a fast runner, and it was said of him that when he got an RBI, he would pass the other runner and get to home plate first. And scratching is not the only instance of Indian medicine being used in the ball games, for just as in the old days with stickball, some Cherokee communities today have more than one ball field, and they do not let the visiting team know which field they will be playing on until time for the game. Even so, there have been instances where an old Cherokee man or woman has been seen strolling around a ball field before the game, smoking.

I know that sports are a major preoccupation of most Americans today. All over Oklahoma I see old, fat, gray-haired men wearing University of Oklahoma shirts, caps, sweat suits, and shoes. It is impossible to negotiate traffic in a town where a university or professional game is being played. There are numerous ESPN channels on television today broadcasting ball games, wrestling, boxing, and other sporting events at all hours of the day. Even so, I know of no other segment of society that is more competitive or more fanatical about sports than the Cherokees. For Cherokees, sports involve all aspects of life, including religion.

Parris

My Cherokee Family

The following essay comes from my untitled and unfinished autobiography.

I want to discuss my Cherokee family, but in order to do so, I have to start out discussing a white man, Richard Pearis. The Pearis name has undergone several spelling changes that I know about, and I am suspicious of several more. I think that it may originally have been the same name as Pearse, which was the name of one of the leaders of the Irish patriots during the 1916 rebellion. Patrick Pearse also spelled his name in Gaelic as Padraig Phiarais or Piarais. It is also interesting to me, although some might find it to be utterly coincidental, that one of Pearse's colleagues was James Connolly (Gaelic, Seamus O'Conghaile), the surname, like all the other variants of Connor, O'Connor, O'Connolly, and so forth, coming from Connacht, meaning "land of the descendants of Conn." By the way, I'm part Irish, but I can't prove it.

Richard Pearis was the son of Irish immigrants to colonial America. In the 1700s, he left his parents in Pennsylvania and went down into the Carolinas, where he obtained a license to trade with the Cherokee Indians. For a time, he was a partner of Nathaniel Gist, who is rumored to have been the father of the great Sequoyah. Richard was married to a daughter of Ama-edohi, town chief of Tellico, who was declared "Emperor of the Cherokees" by the British. Of course, the Cherokees never really knew that. The British called the "emperor" Moytoy. (Richard Pearis also had a white wife back in Charlestown, South Carolina, but that was a fairly common practice among the traders in those days.)

Richard spent enough time among the Cherokees to learn the language (not a mean task), for he is listed as interpreter at several different treaty signings. He is mentioned briefly in the memoirs of both Thomas Jefferson and George Washington, Washington writing, while still an officer in the British army, "Captain Pearis came into my office and threw three fresh scalps on my desk." He did not say whose scalps they were. I assume they were either those of Frenchmen or of Indians who were members of tribes allied to the French.

When the colonists in Virginia wanted to persuade the Cherokees to join them in a war against the French, they sent Pearis and his partner to try to win them over. They did not ask the Cherokees to actually fight the French, but instead to fight the French allies, the Shawnees. During talks in the council house, Richard Pearis held up his account book for all to see. The book contained the names of all the Cherokees who owed him money. In a grand gesture, he tossed the book into the fire. The Cherokees decided to fight the Shawnees.

Richard Pearis was also present at the negotiations for the sale of Kentucky by the Cherokees to the Transylvania Land Company, a sale that was in violation of a royal proclamation as well as of an agreement some Cherokees had signed in England. The great Cherokee war leader Dragging Canoe spoke out against the sale, and Richard Pearis joined him in that protest. I shall always be proud of him for that. The old men of the tribe, however, prevailed, and the sale was concluded. The American Revolution broke out soon after that.

Pearis was a Loyalist, a Tory, and throughout the Revolution remained with the faction of Cherokees led by Dragging Canoe and allied with Great Britain. They became known as Chickamaugas or Chickamauga Cherokees. When the war came to an end, Pearis fled the country, moving to the Bahamas. He left behind his Cherokee wife (whose name, as far as I can tell, has not been recorded, although some Pearis descendants, genealogists, say that it was "Pratchy," a very un-Cherokee-sounding name) and a son, George. Pearis lived into his nineties and died in the Bahamas. Although I do not know, I have always assumed that he had a third family there.

Left in the Cherokee Nation, George changed the spelling of his last name from "Pearis" to "Paris." He became the captain of a contingent of the Cherokee Light Horse, the national police. He was also apparently fairly prosperous. His son was named Robert, and Robert's son was Robert, Jr. During the pressures for Cherokee removal from Georgia in the 1830s, Robert, Sr., and Robert, Jr., moved west with their families to Arkansas, and later moved across the line into what is now Oklahoma. The Trail of Tears, of course, followed shortly afterward, in 1838 and 1839, and nearly all Cherokees were relocated there. Robert, Jr.'s son, Robert Malachi Parris, was my great-grandfather. (Somewhere along the line, someone added another "r" to the surname.) He graduated from the Cherokee Male Seminary, the first institution of higher learning west of the Mississippi River, in 1887, became a teacher, a storekeeper, and a postmaster. He was very fond of the poetry of Lord Byron. Grandma said that because his father died before he was born, he could cure babies of the thrush by breathing into their mouths, and mothers with sick infants brought them from all around for that purpose. As Robert, Jr., had died young, Robert M. was raised by a stepfather, Aaron Crittenden.

My grandmother, Myrtle, grew up on her allotment outside of Hulbert, Indian Territory (now Oklahoma). She attended the Cherokee Female Seminary in Tahlequah but did not graduate. Even so, she became a teacher in Cherokee Nation schools. My grandfather, Benjamin Franklin Conley, was also a teacher, and I'm not sure, but I think that may have been how they met. She told me long after he was gone that the only reason she married him was to keep him from getting drunk again and going to town to shoot out all the streetlights.

Grandma believed that there had been a tradition in the family to carry on the name "Robert Parris," but that her father had been unable to do so. Because of that, when my father was born, she named him Robert Parris Conley. I don't know what took her so long to get around to it, as he was her youngest son and the ninth of ten children. At any rate, he was obviously her favorite. She often baked two apple pies, one for the family and one for him. When Grandma married B. F. Conley, she pretty much removed herself from her Cherokee community. Grandpa had ambitions, and they led him away from home, seeking jobs, to Arkansas, Missouri, Oklahoma City, and eventually to Okmulgee as railway express agent. Grandma was already somewhat removed from her own family. Her father had died when she was only ten years old, and she was raised by a stepfather, Richard Hinton. Her father's father had died before his son was born, and so Robert M. was raised by a stepfather, Crittenden. Estranged from her own family and from her Cherokee community, Grandma's life became her husband and children.

They lived in Okmulgee for years, and Okmulgee, in the Creek Nation, became "home" for all of us. That was where the family gathered when I was a child. My aunts and uncles and cousins would all show up at the same time, and kids would sleep on pallets all over the floor. Our connections to the Cherokee Nation came from listening to the stories my grandparents would tell. There were lots of stories, stories about the Wickliffes, about Ned Christie, about Zeke and Dick Crittenden, who Grandma called her cousins. There were stories about teaching school in the old Indian Territory days, and there were Grandma's stories about being a student in the Cherokee Female Seminary. I almost lived for those stories.

Beyond the stories at my grandparents' house, there was reading, if one could ever find such tales in books. There was S. J. Harman's *Hell on the Border,* and when I was thirteen or fourteen years old, *True West* magazine appeared on the scene. Now and then it would publish something about the Indian Territory days. As the years went by, I found more and more books to read, but that was really my whole connection to the Cherokee Nation or Cherokee people for a good many years. When I finished my master's degree, I went out into the wicked world to teach, and I ended up at Northern Illinois University (NIU). I hated it. I got to thinking more and more about home, and when I did, I thought about the past for some reason.

So I was thinking about Indian Territory and about the Cherokee Nation and about the stories I'd grown up listening to from my grandparents. I started looking for more material in print, and I started writing about the things I had learned. I got especially irritated and frustrated when I ran across stories about Ned Christie, who was universally regarded as a bad outlaw, the worst, in fact, according to at least one source, to ever infest the Indian Territory. I wanted to write something about Ned Christie, but I was unable to come up with the right research material, so instead, I wrote a novel, and that launched my somewhat dubious career as a writer.

I went from NIU to Southwest Missouri State University, and from there I endured a year of unemployment. To get through that year, I went back to Wichita Falls, Texas, where I had finished school. Toward the end of that year, I assume because of my publications, I received a letter from the dean at Eastern Montana College (EMC) in Billings, asking me to apply for a position there called Coordinator of Indian Culture. I applied and got the job.

While I was at EMC, I received a copy of the Cherokee Nation's newspaper calling for registration of Cherokee voters. I registered and voted in the first election. Then I got another issue of the paper that included a letter from the new chief. Ross Swimmer, for whom I did not vote, put out a call for all qualified Cherokees to come home and work for the Cherokee people. I wrote him a letter, which he turned over to Chad Smith, who was the tribal planner at the time. Chad hired me, and I moved to Tahlequah. At last I had made that connection to Tahlequah, to the Cherokee Nation, to Cherokee communities. I met Evelyn, my wife, there, and although I only worked for the Cherokee Nation for one year, it changed my whole life. It's almost like I started my life over. I've led at least two lives. If I think about it enough, there might have been more.

Old-Time Cherokee Warriors

Charlie Wickliffe, the Army Corps of
Engineers, and the Port of Catoosa

Sometime in the mid-1950s, some big shots in the U.S. Army Corps of Engineers got hold of a copy of Joyce Kilmer's little verse "Trees," and when they read the line that says "only God can make a tree," it made them extremely jealous, for the Army Corps of Engineers thinks that it can make anything. After all, its engineers have made dozens and dozens of lakes where there were no lakes. They held a high-level conference, and their emotions ranged from jealousy to rage and fury. They could get nowhere, however, with the idea of making a tree, so instead of admitting defeat and failure, words not even in their vocabulary, they just sort of shifted gears, sliding the discussion from the making of trees to the creation of seaports.

Anyone can make a seaport where the ocean touches land, one of them said, but not even God had made an inland seaport, a seaport in the middle of a continent. Now that was a thought. That was a worthy task for the big shots in the U.S. Army Corps of Engineers to tangle with, to sink their teeth into, to show the world that they could make anything, something that even God had not made, an inland seaport. (The tree was totally forgotten.)

Sometime in the late 1890s, just prior to Oklahoma statehood, Charlie Wickliffe, full-blood Cherokee, a member of the Nighthawk Keetoowah Society, which was dedicated to the preservation of Cherokee culture and Cherokee sovereignty, and his brothers, John and Tom, killed a deputy U.S. marshal. Just killed him and left him dead. Other deputy marshals came after them for having done that terrible deed. The Wickliffes killed them too. They became wanted men, wanted for the killing of deputy U.S. marshals, nothing else. Everyone wondered why the Wickliffes had killed that first deputy.

Their reasons for killing the rest of them were clear enough, but that first one was a puzzle.

The geniuses in the Army Corps of Engineers finally laid their nefarious plans, and they went to work like an army of ants. They dredged the Arkansas River bed from the Gulf of Mexico through Louisiana and Arkansas into Oklahoma all the way to the little town of Catoosa, a suburb of Tulsa. (Why they did not fix up the levees in New Orleans at that time is a mystery, as most of their inbound goods originate there.) At one point they ploughed into the Verdigris River, and where they did so we no longer have an Arkansas River or a Verdigris River. Instead, we have an Arkansas-Verdigris Navigation Channel (their official name for it now is, I believe, the McClellan-Kerr Arkansas River Navigation System). Finished in 1970, it's a marvelous Army Corps of Engineers achievement, something that even God had never done, and it culminates at the PORT OF CATOOSA! An ocean port at Tulsa, Oklahoma!

I have heard that Charley Wickliffe's mother was a medicine woman, a female Indian doctor, a conjurer. I believe it. Furthermore, I imagine that she could look well into the future and see what was coming way on down the road. There was certainly some powerful medicine at work around Charley, for you know, they searched for him and chased after him for several years, and then they never really caught him. Tom and John went to the authorities after statehood, and told them that Charley was dead. They said that they never really did any killing. Charley had done it all, they said.

The authorities insisted on seeing the body, and so two deputy marshals were assigned to go to the funeral and take a look. The casket was sealed. "Open it up," the deputies demanded. They were told that Charley's face had been bashed in, and they didn't really want to open the casket. The deputies looked at Charley's mother, and at all the other sad-faced mourners, and they shrugged their shoulders and let it go. They went back to their office where they reported that Charley was dead all right, and so the case was officially closed. The folks back at the funeral went ahead and buried the casket, which contained the body of a hog.

So back to the original question: why did Charley kill that first deputy U.S. marshal? Don't you think that his mama had looked into the future? Don't you think that she had given it a long and hard look? Oklahoma had already come into being. The railroad that Principal Chief John Ross had fought against so long and so hard had already come through the Cherokee Nation, bringing with it all the changes and all the riffraff that Ross had said it would bring. Don't you think that she could see what else was coming?

The deputy marshal represented the white people's law and order. He represented the foreign new order that was taking over the Cherokee Nation. He represented the new civilization that was already in the process of replacing the old Cherokee civilization. The white people's civilization would pave the way for all kinds of new atrocities that Mama Wickliffe could foresee: Colonel Sanders chicken, McDonald's hamburgers, superhighways, toll roads, airplanes and airports where you have to wait in long lines and then take off your shoes to take a ride, television sets you have to pay to watch even after you have bought the set, microwave ovens, cell phones stuck on people's ears everywhere you look, computers, iPods, the legalized protection racket called insurance, high taxes to support unconscionable overseas wars, no-smoking signs everywhere you turn, organized crime, and guess what? The Arkansas-Verdigris Navigation Channel and the PORT OF CATOOSA!

Charley was just doing the work of the old Cherokee warriors, defending the old Cherokee way of life against the incursions of white civilization. Charley and Charley's mama tried, but the tide of white people's civilization was just too much for them. It was too little, too late.

Notes

INDIAN CASINOS

1. James Mooney, *Myths of the Cherokees*. Nineteenth Annual Report to the Bureau of American Ethnology (Washington, D.C.: Smithsonian Institution, 1897–98).
2. The figures in this paragraph were gleaned from Wikipedia, the free encyclopedia on the Web (http://en.wikipedia.org/wiki/Native_American_gambling_enterprises). Admittedly, Wikipedia is a questionable source, but then when you're talking about Indian casinos, what source can you trust?

STAND WATIE

1. Mooney, *Myths of the Cherokees*, 515.

ALL INDIANS ARE ALIKE, OR "CHIEFING"

1. Jack Finger, *Cherokee Americans: The Eastern Band of Cherokees in the Twentieth Century* (Lincoln: University of Nebraska Press, 1991), 161–62.

CHEROKEE OUTLAWS

1. Levi Gritts, "The Legend of Keetoowah," quoted in John D. Gillespie, "The Organization of the Nighthawk Keetoowahs among the Cherokees," *Cherokee Nation News*, Tahlequah, July 17, 1973, 4.
2. Mooney, *Myths of the Cherokees*, 239 ff.

3. Henry Dawes's address to the 1885 Lake Mohonk Conference, quoted in "The Indians in the United States," in José Martí, *Selected Writings* (New York: Penguin, 2002).

4. There is much useful information on the Nighthawk Keetoowahs in Janey B. Hendrix, *Redbird Smith and the Nighthawk Keetoowahs* (Park Hill, Okla.: Cross-Cultural Education Center, 1983). The transition from clan law to constitutional law and all that goes with it is well documented in Rennard Strickland, *Fire and the Spirits: Cherokee Law from Clan to Court* (Norman: University of Oklahoma Press, 1975). Glenn Shirley has done an admirable job of detailing the criminal cases of Judge Isaac Parker in *Law West of Fort Smith* (Lincoln: University of Nebraska Press, 1968). Tom Starr was written about by Helen Starr Thrasher in "The Blood of a Hundred Men," *True West* (May–June 1972). Bill Pigeon was covered by Robert F. Turpin in "Cherokee Bill Pigeon," *Great West* 5, no. 3 (June 1971), and by Jack F. Kilpatrick in "The Cherokees Remember Their Badmen" *True West* (August 1969). One of the spurious tales of Mose Miller can be found in Jack Forbes, "Mose Miller: Mad Killer of the Cookson Hills," *The West* (September 1964); another appears in W. F. Jones, *The Experiences of a Deputy U.S. Marshal of the Indian Territory*, probably published by Jones in Tulsa in 1937. Paul I. Wellman, among many others, presented the standard Ned Christie story in *A Dynasty of Western Outlaws* (New York: Doubleday, 1961), and Howard Newberry wrote about the Wickliffes in "Manhunt in the Spavinaws," *Frontier Times* (October–November 1967). At long last, carefully researched and well-documented versions of the Ned Christie story were written and published by Philip Steele, *The Last Cherokee Warriors* (Gretna, La.: Pelican Publishing, 1974), and by Bonnie Stahlman Speer, *The Killing of Ned Christie* (Norman, Okla.: Reliance Press, 1990).

GRAFTERS, SOONERS, AND OTHER CROOKS

1. Angie Debo, *And Still the Waters Run: The Betrayal of the Five Civilized Tribes* (New York: Gordian Press, 1966), 92.

CHEROKEE WOMEN AND THE CLAN SYSTEM

1. Donald Day, *Will Rogers: A Biography* (New York: David McKay, 1962), 3.

CHEROKEE LITERATURE

1. James W. Parins, *John Rollin Ridge: His Life and Works* (Lincoln: University of Nebraska Press, 1991).

2. Daniel F. Littlefield, Jr., and James W. Parins, eds., *Native American Writing in the Southeast: An Anthology, 1875–1935* (Jackson: University of Mississippi Press, 1995).

CHEROKEE NAMES

1. Charles Hudson, *The Southeastern Indians* (Knoxville: University of Tennessee Press, 1976), 325.

WILL ROGERS

1. The sources for this essay include: Jerome Beatty, *Will Rogers* (Akron, Ohio: Saalfield, 1935); Day, *Will Rogers*; Bryan B. Sterling, ed., *The Will Rogers Scrapbook* (New York: Bonanza Books, 1976); Richard M. Ketchum, *Will Rogers: The Man and His Times* (New York: American Heritage, 1976); Arthur Frank Wertheim and Barbara Bair, eds., *The Papers of Will Rogers*, Vols. 1–5 (Norman: University of Oklahoma Press, 1996–2006).

THE FREEDMEN CONTROVERSY

1. R. Halliburton, Jr., *Red over Black: Black Slavery among the Cherokee Indians* (Westport, Conn.: Greenwood Press, 1977); Daniel F. Littlefield, Jr., *The Cherokee Freedman: From Emancipation to American Citizenship* (Westport, Conn.: Greenwood Press, 1978).

2. Halliburton, *Red over Black*, 7.

3. Halliburton, *Red over Black*, 14.

4. Halliburton, *Red over Black*, 37.

5. Rachel Carolyn Eaton, *John Ross and the Cherokee Indians* (Menasha, Wis.: George Banta, 1914).
6. Littlefield, *Cherokee Freedman*, 29.
7. Littlefield, *Cherokee Freedman*, 51.
8. *Cherokee Phoenix*, April 2007.

KEETOOWAH

1. Georgia Rae Leeds, *The United Keetoowah Band of Cherokee Indians in Oklahoma* (New York: Peter Lang, 1996), 6.

THE DRAGGING CANOE— NANCY WARD CONTROVERSY

1. Mooney, *Myths of the Cherokee*, 43.

CALIFORNIA CHEROKEES

1. Russell Thornton, *The Cherokees: A Population History* (Lincoln: University of Nebraska Press, 1990), 148.
2. E. Raymond Evans, "Following the Rainbow: The Cherokees in the California Gold Fields," *Journal of Cherokee Studies* (Winter 1977): 170–75.

CHEROKEES AND SPORTS

1. Mooney, *Myths of the Cherokees*, 286–87.
2. Hudson, *Southeastern Indians*, 411.
3. Mooney, *Myths of the Cherokees*, 422.
4. Rodney Leftwich, *Arts and Crafts of the Cherokee*, Cuyllowhee, N.C.: Land of the Sky Press, 1970, 119.
5. Hudson, *Southeastern Indians*, 425, 426.

Index

Abolitionism, 26
Adair, James, 180
Adair, John Lynch, 92
Amateur Athletic Union (AAU), 182
Anetsa, 176
Anetsagi, 176
Army Corps of Engineers, 190
Athletes, 182. *See also* individual sports; Sports, Cherokees and
Attack on Watauga settlements, 158

Baseball, 182. *See also* individual sports; Sports, Cherokees and
Beloved Woman. *See* Ward, Nancy
Bering Strait migration, 51
Birchfield, Donnie, 6, 14
Blood, Cherokee, 33. *See also* Citizenship
Boomers, 66–69. *See also* Oklahoma Sooners
Boudinot, Elias, 18, 19, 111; death of, 57; literary works of, 90. *See also* Watie, Stand
Boudinot, Frank, 97, 147
Brant, Chief Joseph, 36
Bureau of Indian Affairs (BIA), 12, 155
Busyhead, Dennis Wolfe, 140

California Cherokees, 161–63
Cards, 151–53. *See also* Games
Casinos, 6–14; income from, 13; and tribal citizenship, 33
Catoosa, Port of. *See* Port of Catoosa
Celebrities, Cherokee, 96–101
Certificate of Degree of Indian Blood (CDIB), 151
Cherokee Bill, 50, 55
Cherokee Kid, The. *See* Rogers, Will
Cherokee Nation: California, 161–63; casinos, 11; citizenship in, 33–39; constitution (1839), 136; division of, 41; enterprises, 13; history of, 50–54; literature of, 87–95; names, 114–20; Oklahoma, history of in, 40–44; removal of, 53; separation of, 25; sports, 174–84; warriors, 190–92; women and the clan system, 75–80
Cherokee National Female Seminary, 130
Cherokee National Prison, 130
Cherokee National Supreme Court building, 130
Cherokee Phoenix, 13, 20, 100, 111, 133

Cherokee Removal (1838-39), 131
Chiefing, 45–48
Christie, Ned, 49, 55, 62–65, 146; in
 historical fiction, 165–66
Citizenship, 33–39
Civil War: Cherokee Nation
 involvement in, 42; Cherokee
 outlaws during, 56–58; and
 Freedmen controversy, 133–44;
 and Stand Watie, 26–29
Clan system, women and the,
 75–80
Confederate Cherokees, 27
Conley, Benjamin Franklin, 15,
 49–50
Conley, Gene, 182
Conley, John, 181
Constitution, Cherokee Nation
 (1839), 136
Creek War, 19
Crittenden, Dick, 50
Curtis, Edward, 46
Curtis Act, 148

Daltons, the, 63, 84, 146
Daughters of the American Revo-
 lution (DAR), 70–74
Davis, William, 138
Dawes, Henry, 54, 59
Dawes Act, 54
Dawes Commission, 36–38
Dawes Roll, 140, 143, 151
Debo, Angie, 11, 66, 148
De Soto, Hernando, 51
Dick, Cecil, 17
Digadayosdi, 180
Dragging Canoe, 70, 78, 89–90, 96;
 in historical fiction, 165; Nancy
 Ward and, 158–60; Richard
 Pearis and, 186

English names, 119. *See also*
 Names, Cherokee

Federal Bureau of Investigation
 (FBI), 12
Five Civilized Tribes, 42, 53,
 110–13
Foxwoods Casino, 13
Freedmen controversy, 133–44

Gal'kaliski, 118
Gamblers, 6–7; origin of gatayusti,
 7–10
Games, 7, 177. *See also* Casinos;
 individual sports; Sports,
 Cherokees and
Gatayusti, origin of, 7–10
General Allotment Act, 43, 54
Gideon, Oklahoma, 16
Gilstrap, United States marshal,
 15, 49
Gist, Nathaniel, 185
Gold rush, California, 161
Goldsby, Crawford. *See* Cherokee
 Bill
Great Depression, 125, 162
Gulager, Clu, 99, 163

Haskell Institute, 106
Hollywood, depiction of Indians,
 45–48
Humor, Indian, 102–109

Indian Gaming Regulatory Act
 (IGRA), 11

Jackson, Andrew, 19, 41, 52, 118,
 123
James, Jesse, 62, 84, 146
Jefferson, Thomas, 41, 52

Keetoowah, North Carolina,
154–57
Keetoowah Society, 61–65, 155
Kennedy, Henry, 144
Ketchum, Richard, 122
King, Richard, 35, 106, 153
Knights of the Golden Circle, 26

Lee, Robert E., 27
Legal system, 54–56
Literature of Cherokee Nation,
87–95
Looney Bear, 15
Louisiana Purchase, 41

Mafia, involvement with casinos,
10
Mankiller, Wilma, 97, 162
Maples, Dan, 63, 64, 146
McMurtry, Larry, 165
Miller, Mose, 49, 63
Mixed-bloods, 52
Mooney, James, 7, 18, 51, 88, 174,
179
Moravian Mission school, 19

Names, Cherokee, 114–20
Nicknames, 114
Nighthawk Keetoowahs, 61–65,
155, 190
Nixon, Richard, 43, 151
Norton, John, 36

Oconostota, 77, 96
Oklahoma, 40–44; Indian casinos,
6; Nighthawk Keetoowahs, 62;
statehood, 54
Oklahoma Sooners, 40, 66–69
Oskison, John, 94, 145–50, 164
Outlaws, Cherokee, 49–65

Owl, Sampson, 181
Ox Heart, 68

Parins, James W., 91
Parris, origin of name, 185–89
Pearis, Richard, 70, 185–89
Pigeon, Bill, 50, 59, 60, 64, 170
Pin Indians, 155
Port of Catoosa, 190–92
Proctor, Zeke, 50, 59, 60, 64, 165;
trial of, 61

Rattling Gourd, Ellis, 50
Reconstruction Treaty. *See* Treaty
of 1866
Red Stick War, 19
Relocation programs (1950s), 162
Removal Act of 1830, 41
Ridge, John Rollin, 57, 161; literary
works of, 90
Ridge, Major, 19; murder of, 22;
and murder of Elias Boudinot,
21; as plantation owner, 135
Rogers, Clement Vann, 55
Rogers, Roy, 48
Rogers, Will, 6, 55, 78, 103, 121–28,
147; as athlete, 181; move to
California, 163
Ross, John, 19, 42, 57, 97, 129; Civil
War, 137

Saunooke, Osley Bird, 181
Sequoyah, 50, 56, 100, 167–68
Shoe Boot, 135
Sioux Indians, 45
Sixkiller, Sam, 50
Slavery, 133. *See also* Freedmen
controversy
Smith, Archilla, 22
Smith, Chad, 13, 33, 133, 144, 189

Snell, Charles ("Chug"), 107, 119
Snell, Evelyn, 115, 166
Snell, Swimmer Wesley, 115, 184
Sooners. *See* Oklahoma Sooners
Sports, Cherokees and, 174–84
Starr, Belle, 58, 82, 86
Starr, Henry, 58, 62, 81–86, 97, 103
Starr, James, 24, 57, 82
Swimmer, George Washington, 55

Tahlequah, Oklahoma, 17, 41, 53, 130, 155
Tecumseh, 148
Thornton, Joe, 99, 181
Trail of Tears, 20, 21, 53, 56, 131. *See also* Oklahoma
Treaty of 1866, 29–32, 138, 142. *See also* Watie, Stand
Treaty of New Echota, 20
Treaty Party, 12, 20, 53, 56
Tribes: identification of, 34; sovereignty of, 43; specific historic fiction of, 164–73. *See also* Five Civilized Tribes
Tsiyu-Gansini. *See* Dragging Canoe

Ukitena, 88, 170
Uluhsadi, 170

Unassigned Lands, 67
United Keetoowah Band of Cherokee Indians in Oklahoma (UKB), 11; 155–57
University of Oklahoma, 68. *See also* Oklahoma Sooners
U.S. government, jurisdiction in Indian Territory, 59
U.S. Supreme Court, 11

Vann, Marilyn, 141–44

Wannabes, 33–39
Ward, Nancy, 75, 77–80, 134; Dragging Canoe and, 158–60
Warriors, Cherokee, 190–92
Watie, Charles, 162
Watie, John, 162
Watie, Stand, 18–32, 97; and Civil War, 137
Wickliffe, Charley, 15–17, 49, 64, 190–92
Wickliffe, George, 157
Wickliffe, John, 16, 49, 64, 190
Wickliffe, Tom, 16, 49, 64, 190
Women, Cherokee and the clan system, 75–80
Woyi, Wili. *See* Pigeon, Bill
Writers, Cherokee, 87–95